Lives from a Black Tin Box

Prudence Bell grew up in Devon not too far from her grand-father, the son of Herbert and Elizabeth. She moved to Wales on her husband's ordination into the Church in Wales. She has three grown-up children and has been involved with various ministries over the last 40 years, whilst also serving as a magistrate.

Dr Ronald Clements and his family moved to Fujian Prov-ince, China, in 1986, where Ronald lectured in Civil Engin-eering. He is now a full-time writer and researcher, living in Kent. He writes Christian biographies and resource materials, and directs and writes scripts for TV documentaries and video promotions. ronaldclements.com

'In this luminous little book, we have the history of a family whose heroic faith and service led them eventually to martyrdom in China in the terrible days of the Boxer Rebellion – a history written by a member of the same family, with obvious love and gratitude. Readers will share that love and gratitude as they read of how Elizabeth and Herbert left behind the secure world of Victorian Wales and England and put their gifts and skills at the service of the gospel in China. The story is told vividly and compellingly; and it is told in the light of the extraordinary expansion of Christian faith in China in recent decades. As always, God honours the deaths of his saints; and the literally world-changing potential of the gospel in China today owes so much, humanly speaking, to those who, like Herbert and Elizabeth, launched out into the deep for the sake of Christ.'

Archbishop Rowan Williams – Master of Magdalene College, Cambridge; former Archbishop of Canterbury

'What a story! Prudence has written the enthralling story of her visit to the place in China where her great-grandparents were murdered. They were medical missionaries, caught in the conflict of the Boxer Rising and the horrific persecution of the Chinese Christian church early in the last century. Prudence has carefully pieced together their amazing story from family memorabilia and added a wealth of fascinating period and cultural detail. She has not only brought this brave couple "back to life" but, because of her visit to the church they founded in China, she is able to celebrate the wonderful fruit which followed their tragic deaths.'

Jennifer Rees Larcombe – author; Beauty from Ashes Healing Ministry

'This book movingly describes the lives of two humble missionaries who laid down their lives for Christ during the Boxer Rebellion in north China over a century ago. It beautifully traces God's purposes from the quiet nonconformist chapels of Wales to the turbulent scenes of a late 19th century China riven by poverty, rebellion and superstition and shows clearly how the tremendous growth of the church in China in recent years was born out of the sacrifice and martyrdom of western missionaries, still honoured by Chinese believers today.'

Tony Lambert – Director of Research,
OMF International; author, *China's Christian Millions*

'Based on remarkably vivid contemporary documents, *Lives from a Black Tin Box* is a gripping narrative of hope and tragedy, love and violence, faith and hatred, conflict and resolution. It is set against epic events – the 19th century entanglements of China with the West and the brutal Boxer Rebellion – but it is an intimate, moving human story, suffused with the religious optimism of the couple at its centre. In the end, it is also a story about history itself – what is lost in the storm of terrible events and what, against all expectation, somehow survives.'

Fintan O'Toole – Assistant Editor, *The Irish Times*

'Prudence Bell's words riveted listeners when we first used them on the BBC Radio Wales programme *All Things Considered*. Speaking into her mini tape recorder, her voice shaking with emotion, she had just visited the exact place in China where her great-grandparents had been killed for their faith: "I feel dreadful as I stand here and think how brave they were."

'The story of how Prudence and her husband found that site of martyrdom and met a flourishing Christian congregation made compelling listening. I'm delighted that it's now here in much greater detail.

'In part, this book is a colourful family memoir, reaching from the western tip of Wales to the east end of London, and then on to the Congo and China. It's an easy-to-read, engaging piece of research. More importantly, it's a challenge to anyone who believes that authentic mission can ever be without cost. Or that martyrdom is ever the end of the story.'

Revd Roy Jenkins – BBC broadcaster; Baptist minister

'This is both an encouraging and challenging read – resurrection following a sacrificial carrying of the cross of Christ, from tiny beginnings in Wales to a thriving church in China. The author's own connection with the story makes her visit to China especially poignant, as she is able to embrace those whose ancestors had martyred hers. It made me wonder how ready we are to carry the cost of taking the Gospel to people groups in the UK who have never heard of Jesus' saving love. I hope that others will profit from this book as much as I have done.'

Canon Dr Christina Baxter CBE – former Principal, St John's College, Nottingham

'A fascinating cameo of family and missionary history, culminating in the events of the Boxer Rebellion. Culminating?

No! For God had a remarkable postscript in store for the Dixons' great-granddaughter Prudence. With God, tragedy can never be the final word . . .'

Sheila Walker – author,
Contemporary Reflections for Praying and Preaching

'As a Chinese Christian, I have been researching the Xinzhou martyrs for more than 14 years. Elizabeth and Herbert Dixon are heroic names in Chinese missionary history. The reason is more than the blood they shed in 1900. When they were preaching the gospel and making disciples among Chinese people in Xinzhou, Shanxi, they first made themselves disciples and servants of our Lord Jesus. Carrying their crosses, they followed Jesus Christ, thus they walked into historic China and are still walking in modern China. They have never been forgotten by the Chinese people . . .'

Dr Henry Zhang – Associate Professor,
Purdue University, Indiana, USA

'The habit of reading missionary biographies has only recently disappeared from Christian life. Those examples of Christian brothers and sisters who courageously sacrificed everything for the sake of the Gospel have long challenged readers to value their faith more highly and to trust their God more fully. This account of Herbert and Elizabeth Dixon's lives in China provides an excellent example of why the church today needs to recover this lost practice.'

Andrew Kaiser – historian;
researcher of Shanxi Church history

Lives from a Black Tin Box

Prudence Bell and Ronald Clements

Authentic

First published 2014 by Authentic Media Limited
52 Presley Way, Crownhill, Milton Keynes, MK8 0ES.
authenticmedia.uk

British Library Cataloguing in Publication Data
A catalogue record for this book is available from the British Library
ISBN 978-1-86024-931-0   978-1-78078-239-3 (e-book)

Cover design by Peter Barnsley
Printed and bound by CPI Group (UK) Ltd., Croydon, CR0 4YY

For the succeeding generations of this family
that they might not lose sight of their
Christian inheritance.

Contents

Contents

Illustrations

Source of all illustrations listed here: P. Bell

Acknowledgements

This book has benefited from the help and advice of a number of people. Foremost amongst these is Jean Morgan, who has been involved with the project from the beginning, and who has contributed greatly in sourcing material, carrying out research, offering salient insights, and reviewing the work in progress. There are few pages, if any, which have not in some way been enhanced by her input.

We are grateful to family members for their encouragement and support; in particular, Stuart Bell, Julia Bell, Peter Dixon, Anne Clements, Bethan Ellish, Emma Godwin and Shona Clements. Bethan is also to be thanked for her astute skills as editor.

Peter Davies has been very helpful in providing material from his own research into the Williams family history, and we have appreciated the advice of Lyn Dafis on Welsh culture and language. We are also grateful to Professor David Killingray for his expertise on mission in the Congo, and to Dr Henry Zhang, Andrew Kaiser and Eric Chandler for insights into the Baptist Missionary Society activity in Shanxi. Yan Aiwu Angela Wade kindly helped us with the translation of documents in Chinese. We are grateful to Sheila Walker and

Joyce Wallace, who reviewed the book and whose comments have enabled us to improve it before submitting it for publication. Thanks also go to Christine Bromwich, who accompanied Prudence and Stuart to Xinzhou in 2006.

We have spent a great deal of time in the Baptist Missionary Society (BMS) archives at Regent's College, Oxford, and also at the National Library of Wales, at Hackney Archives, and in the library at the School of Oriental and African Studies, London University; all places where the staff have been most helpful. Particular thanks are due to Angela Haley of Otford village library, who has gone well beyond her duties to find the most obscure of books. We are very grateful to Revd David Kerrigan and Mark Craig of BMS for permission to use and quote from BMS archive material and to David for providing the foreword.

Our thanks must also go to Authentic Media, particularly Becky Fawcett and Sheila Jacobs, for their help in publishing this book, and making Elizabeth and Herbert's story available to you and many others.

Finally, Ronald would like to thank the Dixon/Bell family, and Prudence Bell in particular, for generously allowing him access to the many letters and documents relating to Elizabeth and Herbert and for permission to tell their story.

Foreword

The vantage point of history is useful in many ways. The immediate events of the day can be seen in a wider context. The fruitfulness or otherwise of people's life and work can be assessed. And in the calm light of day, lessons can be gleaned and dispassionate reflections shared.

But life is not lived with this degree of objectivity. Decisions have to be made without knowing whether they will bear fruit or not, and as events unfold the heat of the moment is anything but dispassionate.

This is the unique strength of a story recounted through access to the personal letters and diary entries of Elizabeth and Herbert Dixon, missionaries of the Baptist Missionary Society. It's a story that lives and breathes the era in which they lived, and richly chronicles their hopes and fears, the worldview they possessed and the faith that inspired them to live and die in obedience to God's call on their lives.

Today's world is so different that it can be tempting to file this away as an interesting footnote to history, a story with little contemporary relevance. Nothing could be further from the truth.

In today's risk-averse world, the lives of Elizabeth and Herbert do not speak of reckless disregard of life and limb, nor of a dereliction of duty to family life. Instead, they remind us of a way of living that truly puts God in first place and sees the missionary endeavour as of such importance that real sacrifices are sometimes demanded.

It is the intensity of the letters and diary entries that prevent us from escaping the experience of stepping, for a while, into their shoes. Whilst in hiding from the Boxers they receive news of dedicated missionary colleagues and valued Chinese believers, who had already been murdered. They are told of a woman missionary who was killed while protecting a young Chinese girl from a mob that had stormed a mission hospital. This book invites you to imagine what went through their minds when they heard this news.

The events of the Boxer Rebellion were deeply distressing for the families of those who survived, and so too for the BMS. Men, women and children have died on missionary service with us from the earliest days, and on each occasion the mission has had to dig deep and consider afresh its calling to be witnesses to Jesus Christ throughout the world.

And so I commend Prudence in completing this labour of love and sincerely hope that many people in our churches will read it and be inspired again by these heroes of the faith who have gone before. In so doing, we will be reminded that the ongoing responsibility for gospel witness is not to be under- taken lightly but with deep reverence for the past.

I also want our missionaries, present and future, to read this. Thankfully, few are called to give their lives in the way that Elizabeth and Herbert did. But, knowing our missionaries as I do, they are people who see their faith as worth living for, because they know too that it is a faith worthy of dying for. There are parts of the world in which we work today where it is not too difficult to envisage a repeat of these events.

And those of us in mission leadership will gain from this story too. If we are ever tempted to set our sights too low, to walk by fear rather than by faith, Elizabeth and Herbert's story will challenge us not to do so.

Jesus said, 'unless a grain of wheat falls into the earth and dies, it remains just a single grain; but if it dies, it bears much fruit' (John 12:24 NRSV). The growth and vitality of the Chinese Church today owes much to those who gave their lives for its beginning. Amongst them were Elizabeth and Herbert Dixon, for whom we give thanks to God.

David Kerrigan
General Director
BMS World Mission
www.bmsworldmission.org

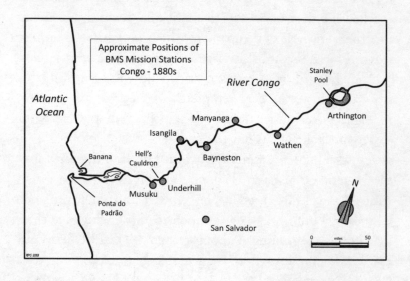

Approximate Positions of
BMS Mission Stations
Congo - 1880s

Atlantic
Ocean

River Congo

Stanley
Pool

Arthington

Manyanga

Isangila

Wathen

Banana

Hell's
Cauldron

Bayneston

Musuku   Underhill

Ponta do
Padrão

San Salvador

N

0   miles   50

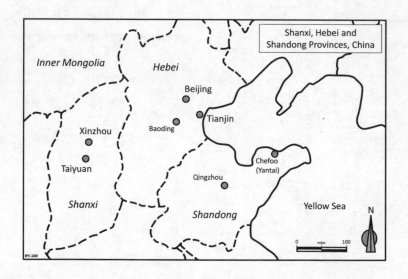

Shanxi, Hebei and
Shandong Provinces, China

Inner Mongolia

Hebei

Beijing

Tianjin

Xinzhou   Baoding

Taiyuan

Chefoo
(Yantai)

Qingzhou

Shanxi

Shandong

Yellow Sea

N

0   miles   100

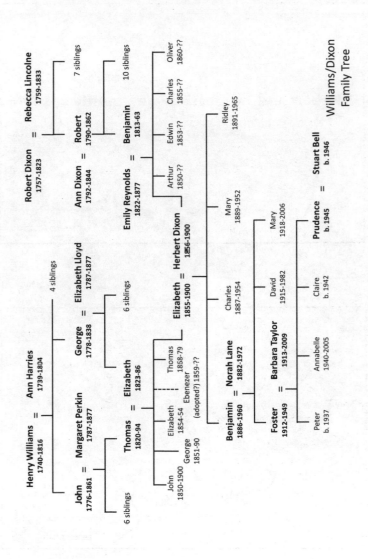

Williams/Dixon
Family Tree

Herbert and Elizabeth Dixon family c. 1898

l to r: Herbert, Mary, Charles, Benjamin,
Ridley, Elizabeth

Prologue

There is a scruffy black tin box that on being opened reveals a diary written on fragile yellowing paper, handwritten letters to four young children from their parents far away in China, sepia Victorian photographs, and browned newspaper cuttings from 1900. This box has been in my family for as long as I can remember.

There are hundreds of digital photos still waiting to be sorted, a black mini tape recorder, a Moleskine journal written in my spidery hand, and painful personal memories, all telling their own tale of my journey to China in October 2006. Tucked into the pocket of the journal is a copy of a photograph from the black box. It fixes in time my great-grandparents, Elizabeth and Herbert Dixon, surrounded by their four children, Benjamin (my grandfather, then aged 12), Charles, Mary and Ridley. This photograph is the first of three images that shape my story and theirs.

The second image remains only in my mind. There is no photo in my collection. Maybe the shock of coming face to face with a larger than life-size portrait of the Chinese Empress Dowager Cixi caused me to forget to take a picture. It was in an exhibition on the small island near the edge of the vast lake in the middle of Yiheyuan, the Summer Palace, which lies on the north-western outskirts of Beijing. As I stood staring at that impassive face, I suddenly became aware that the actions of this woman over a hundred years before had had repercussions on my own life. I was transfixed, feeling as if I was pinned to the ground, yet with the sensation of tumbling down a time tunnel. Shocked, I fought back tears. The journey to trace the life and work of my great-grandparents in China had begun. It was beginning here in Beijing – not, as expected, in a week's time in Taiyuan, Shanxi Province. I stared back into the piercing eyes of a woman who was no longer just a name in a history book, but a real person whose life story connected with mine.

My part in this story came about because of my husband Stuart's long-awaited sabbatical from his ministry as Rector of Aberystwyth. Unexpectedly, we were able to visit China; something I never imagined possible. Expeditions like this depend on the kindness and generosity of others. A friend, Christine Bromwich, who had worked as a teacher in Taiyuan, accompanied us. Zhang, one of her students, gave up a week of his holiday to drive his English teacher and her friends around Shanxi Province. None of us knew, as we squeezed ourselves and our entire luggage into his rather battered, white Ford Fiesta, of the incredible events that lay ahead of us.

Now back home in Aberystwyth, as I prepare to write about these experiences, listening to my tapes and re-reading my journal, I gaze at a photo of Zhang taken in that cramped grey room in Xinzhou city, north of Taiyuan. He is surrounded by members of the local church, all talking excitedly in Mandarin. The photo catches the moment. Zhang sits on the edge of a white plastic chair and waves a bundle of papers at us, repeating over and over again, 'It's a miracle. It's a miracle!'

Three images separated by more than a hundred years – yet the God who transcends time was evidently at work. There is a miraculous connection between that old sepia photograph of my great-grandparents, the overpowering portrait of Empress Dowager Cixi and the picture of excited Zhang, waving those papers in his hand. Later that day in Xinzhou we were able to pray where Elizabeth and Herbert had lived and worked, and where they died – separated from their young family, trapped in the schemes of a dying dynasty, caught up in one of the greatest tragedies that ever befell the Chinese church.

1

A Long Journey

'Thursday's child has far to go . . .'
                                        Traditional nursery rhyme

My great-grandmother, Elizabeth Margaret Williams, was born on a Thursday. And, tragically, she died on a Thursday forty-five years later. So her life was made up of weeks of Thursdays, each providing a small anniversary of her first moments of life, and counting down to that final Thursday when she would be forced to bow, naked, before a mob of armed men and feel the savage blows of a sword across her back and neck.

Elizabeth was born in south-west Wales and murdered at the gates of a remote town in China. It was a long journey for my great-grandmother, from life to death. A journey that started with a sombre two-mile walk – not for her but, stepping seven decades back in time, for *her* great-grand-parents and their children; individuals whose collected lives profoundly influenced the direction of her own.

The Williams family of Treginnis Uchaf was raised out of adversity. In 1784, 8-year-old John and his younger brother, George, stood with their parents on the Pembrokeshire cart track that led towards St David's from Treginnis and watched their home burn. Dark volumes of smoke swirled from the farmhouse's thatched roof. The breeze snatched at burning stalks of straw and deposited them on to the gorse fields, threatening the hedges that marked the margins of their barley crops. Tongues of red flame wrapped themselves around the heavy wooden door and consumed it totally. John showed little emotion. He remained next to his father, not moving, except occasionally to wipe the flecks of soot on his cheeks and forehead into smudges with the sleeve of his shirt. George buried his black hair in his mother's woollen apron and wet the folds he held in his bunched fists with tears. By the time the embers cooled to ashen white, nothing remained of the generous house, the outhouses and their contents, save blackened walls and charred roof beams.

John and George's parents, Henry and Ann Williams, had five children to provide for. The eldest, William, was just in his teens, followed by Thomas and John. George, at 6, was the youngest son. Phebe, the only daughter, was no more than a few months old. Devastated by the loss of their possessions and the business they had worked into a viable concern, the couple sold their few animals, turned their backs on tenant farming and took the dirt road to St David's. It was a familiar path, winding easily around rocky outcrops across the low-lying heathlands of the Treginnis Peninsula; a road travelled on Mondays or Thursdays to market and walked every Sunday to services in the great cathedral. But now it carried only uncertainty. As the young family crossed the narrow River Alun and trudged up the slope into the town, there was nothing for Ann and Henry to do but start again.

Although a city in name, St David's had a meagre reputation. Beyond the grandeur of the church properties and a few substantial stone houses it was, in reality, a poor village. Scattered untidily along two or three unmade roads were a disorderly assortment of cob cottages, crudely constructed with a mixture of compressed straw and clay, smeared with yellowing whitewash and fronted by pigsties. At the top of the hill, Ann and Henry guided their children to one of the houses along the ridge that looks over Glyn Rhosyn, the Vale of Roses, and back towards Treginnis. This was to be Ann and Henry's home for the rest of their lives.

Furniture was begged or borrowed from extended family. The routines of life were re-established. A daily diet of *cawl*, a vegetable broth with a little meat, oatcakes and barley bread were prepared over peat fires in the kitchen on an open hearth. The weekly laundry was taken down to the river and beaten against a stone with a wooden *golchbren* – a heavy utensil made of ash, not dissimilar to a cricket bat – and the clothes lain over gorse bushes to dry.

The house was basic, of rough construction with earthen floors and pinched windows of thick squares of glass, which barely allowed the late afternoon sun to warm the living area. More important, however, was the apparently insignificant mud-walled outhouse at the front of the property. Here lay the family's future prosperity. Ann Williams, determined to provide for her children, opened a shop. It was probably the first in the town, since it became known as 'Old Shop'; a small enterprise that sold basic groceries – currants, rice, salt, sugar, and a luxury item – tea.

Henry and Ann were keen that their children should receive a good education. George's first encounters with education, however, were not a success. He resented the restrictions of the classroom after the freedoms of the farm. He was not aided by the prevailing attitude of the parents of his fellow pupils. Attendance was seasonal. A boy was better employed to help keep the family in food and clothing than sitting behind a rickety table in a spartan room learning to read and write. Few children managed more than a year's tuition, and even when they were in school, truancy proved an attractive alternative. The ruins of the Bishop's Palace opposite the cathedral provided a warren of hiding places. Hours could be spent poaching fat, tame trout from the shallows of the river. And there were otters to be spotted and bird nests to find. Who wouldn't rather climb cliffs or explore the edges of their world?

The day George joined his friends on a truancy expedition he learned an enduring lesson; his parents did not share the popular perceptions of the society in which they lived. By the evening George had not returned home. A search party was anxiously arranged and George was brought back to Old Shop. Henry Williams was livid. His ill-controlled temper was unleashed and George had to listen until his father's fury was spent. 'Thou shalt not miss school' was a command of biblical proportions. George was removed from the ill-disciplined private school he attended and enrolled at the cathedral school. The lesson was learned and he became an outstanding student.

It was also at the cathedral that George found the faith of his fathers. The family had a strong Christian heritage; George's great-grandfather had been a lay vicar. The school provided the foundation for his beliefs with its unyielding emphasis on the learning of catechisms and Bible reading. The services, held in the breathtaking upper nave beneath one of the south arches, established an awe of God. A whisper of prayer sealed a deep-rooted devotion to Christ. Never lukewarm in a commitment, George set his heart on becoming a minister.

In February 1797, aged 18 or 19, George went missing again. Four French ships under the guise of British flags had made a landing on the north Pembrokeshire coast. Seventeen boatloads of troops armed with gunpowder and grenades encamped on the shore west of Fishguard. The French forces were intent on securing a foothold on Welsh soil. George had no hesitation in joining the fight to repel them. A night was spent around the hot forge of the local blacksmith casting bullets made with lead obtained from the cathedral. And then George was off, hurrying on foot the fifteen miles to Fishguard to defend the realm. His distraught family sent one of his brothers to bring him back.

George was gone for two days, caught up in the melee of local farmers and craftsmen, who had turned up in the town with a crude catalogue of weaponry, from pitchforks to guns, all eager to join the regular troops. For twenty-four hours, the two armies defied each other. Tensions ran high. Minor skirmishes took half a dozen lives. Fortunately for George, French morale failed first. The teenager was eventually found marching a group of miserable prisoners to Haverfordwest and persuaded to return home.

Conflict was not confined to the defence of Wales. Around the corner from Old Shop, at the far end of Gospel Lane, was a fellowship of nonconformist believers meeting in a Calvinistic

Methodist chapel built in 1788. George's elder brother, John, establishing his independence from family tradition, started to attend their services. The new chapel had its attractions. There were emotive revivalist preachers to listen to. The services had a more informal air, and Welsh was the language spoken. When his mother also dared to cross the denominational divide, the family split – father against mother, brother against brother. George took the fight to John, literally. The quarrel was violent. An unseemly brawl ensued. Punches were thrown. When the two combatants were forced apart, breathing heavily and still exchanging opinions, there was blood on their knuckles and bruising on their faces.

Perversely, George's rage against the Methodists lasted no more than a year. The simpler entrenched Welshness of the nonconformists captivated him and he found the energy and drive of their pastors invigorating. He discovered a freedom for debate and discussion and felt increasingly drawn to their gatherings. Once again George incurred the wrath of his father.

'You may as well become a tinker!' stormed Henry Williams, when George informed him of his decision to leave the cathedral congregation.

The argument burned on remorselessly. Life at Old Shop became insufferable. John moved to Clegyr Isaf, a strip-field farm out on the low hills east of the town. George, as always the more impulsive of the brothers, decided on a career in colonial India, and applied for a post as a personal secretary.

And here, it appears, God stepped into the story.

George settled himself onto the hard benches of the Methodist chapel. He was there to say his final goodbyes. This was to be his last opportunity to worship in Welsh. As the congregation gathered around him, he told them of his plans. In a few days he would be aboard ship, bound for a voyage around the southern cape of Africa and across the Indian Ocean. He expected never to return to the land of his fathers.

The preacher was an unpolished but effective evangelist by the name of Robert Dafydd, who had travelled from north Wales. He announced his Old Testament passage for the day: Ruth, chapter one – the story of a young foreign widow determined to remain with her mother-in-law, while her mother-in-law pleads with her to stay with her own people.

'Stay.'

The word held him.

George was convinced that it was God's message to him.

In the course of a few minutes the impulses that had propelled him towards India were subdued. God had spoken. George would remain in Wales. It was as well for me that he did, for George was my great-grandmother Elizabeth's maternal grandfather, and though he died long before she was born, the decision he made that Sunday had a crucial influence on both the fortunes and spirituality of the Williams family.

George was unwilling to return to Old Shop. He travelled north to the town of Newcastle Emlyn and became a schoolmaster. But, after two years, ill health forced him to step down. He moved south, this time to Carmarthen, where he found better paid employment as a trader and took pleasure in friendships with the well-educated men of the town. That position was similarly short-lived. In 1804, Ann Williams died and there was no one to manage Old Shop.

'You must return home!' his brothers insisted.

'I'm settled here,' protested George. 'My earnings are good.'

William and John would not countenance abandoning their farms. George's other brother, Thomas, was a cabinet maker and equally vehement that he was not willing to give up his trade.

'I've my own friends here,' George objected.

'You know Mother was the one who kept the store. Father is no businessman.'

'Well, there's a good reason not to go back,' said George. 'Our quarrel is not over.'

George's protests were futile. His brothers were adamant. George had the fewest commitments, the experience, and he was the youngest son. The differences of church and chapel must be put to one side. There was no other option.

'You'll be running Old Shop, then?' Henry asked.

'Yes.'

'And you'll be living here?'

'Yes.'

Henry Williams nodded. The death of his wife had quenched some of his fire. There would be no argument from him. Each Sunday father and son would go their separate ways: Henry down the hill to the cathedral and George up the lane to the chapel. But from Monday to Saturday they would live together at peace.

Old Shop had remained little more than a village store under his mother's oversight. But George, now 26, was not content with that. He diversified into drapery and became a purveyor of candles and an ironmonger. He added butter and barley to his inventory. As George's wealth grew, so did the ever-widening circles of his influence. He leased a windmill on the edge of the town, purchased two granaries and invested in property. His interests encompassed the local port at Porthclais, a narrow winding creek which afforded shelter for eight to ten coastal ships. George improved the quay facilities and established himself as a limeburner, using the large stone kilns that still sit at the head of the harbour. And, finally, he bought boats to carry his reputation beyond the boundaries of the Treginnis Peninsula along the south Wales coast and into Bristol. By the age of 57, George Williams was the owner of 'the only respectable shop in the City',[1] the town's principal merchant, and responsible for all the trade passing out of the harbour mouth at Porthclais.

George's rise to affluence was aided by his wife, Elizabeth Lloyd of Llys-y-frân, a village eighteen miles east of St David's, whom he married in 1810. The couple had seven children – two girls and five boys. George never fulfilled his desire to become a minister, an aspiration subsequently fulfilled by one of his sons (my great-grandmother Elizabeth's favourite uncle, also named George). His faith, nonetheless, was very evident. He strode around the increasingly prosperous streets of the town with a Bible under his arm, and was frequently found in a sheltered spot out in the countryside reading its pages.

When the decision was made to move the Calvinistic Methodist chapel to a location on Ship Street (now Goat Street) in 1817, George provided much of the finance and had his brother, John, sail through a severe storm to fetch wood for the construction from Liverpool. The colossal presence of the new building on the ridge presided over the houses of Ship Street in the same way that the cathedral dominated the River Alun valley. George's devotion to the 'Tabernacle Chapel' was rewarded when he was appointed one of the *blaenoriaid*, a church elder. After the Sunday evening service, visiting preachers were as likely as not to be invited to George's home. When supper was finished, conversation beneath the darkened oak beams of the living room quickly turned to matters of faith. These discussions lasted comfortably into the early hours of Monday morning, until the yellow, smoky flames of the tallow candles finally flickered out. There is no doubt that the Christian environment in which my great-grandmother Elizabeth was nurtured arose from the enduring example of her grandfather, George Williams.

John, the quiet farmer on the hill, although he did not have the trading acumen of George, inherited the ability of his father to nurture his farming business. John outlived his more enterprising brother by twenty-three years. Before his death in 1861, he had accumulated fifty acres of land, a good-sized farm for the time, and employed two labourers and a youth at Clegyr Isaf. Like George, he and his family were members at the Tabernacle Chapel, and it was here, no doubt, that John's elder son, Thomas, and George's younger daughter, Beth, exchanged shy glances across the barn-like sanctuary. It was not long before the local *gwahoddwr*, the 'bidder', was employed to announce the forthcoming marriage of the two cousins. Clad in a white apron and matching ribbon in the buttonhole of his coat, the bidder set out along the lanes of St David's, collecting wedding gifts of barley, cheese, potatoes and turnips in the bag slung across his back.

NOTE

[1] 'Report of the Commissioners on Municipal Corporations in England and Wales, 1835', quoted in P. Davies, *The Footsteps of Our Fathers: Tales of Life in Nineteenth Century St. David's* (St David's: Merrivale, 1994), p. 38. Used with permission: P. Davies.

2

Judging the Future by the Past

'I know no way of judging of the future, but by the past.'
Patrick Henry, 1775[1]

At the heart of St David's lies neither the cathedral nor the chapel, but a square pyramid of worn stone steps on which stands a slender Celtic cross. These days it is fronted by carefully cropped gardens and hemmed in by paving slabs. But in the mid-1800s it dominated the western skyline, standing imposingly alone. Each sunlit day, then as now, the shadow of the cross crept steadily from west to east, marking the daily anniversaries of time.

In the early afternoon of 14 June 1855, this medieval silhouette pointed to what for many years had been the largest house on Cross Square. Set well back from the road was an impressive two-storey, stone-built house named Old Cross. It was a well-proportioned building, with a tiled roof, and two tiers of tall narrow windows cut into its whitewashed front. The property indulged in the opulence of a front garden of small shrubs protected by an ironwork fence and gate. That Thursday there would be few in the town that were not aware that Beth Williams, wife of Thomas, had given birth to a baby girl at Old Cross. They had seen the midwife arrive. The local women were already in their kitchens preparing a gift of bread or butter or sugar for when they went to visit in the next few days. The town was busy with the news – my great-grandmother had begun her journey.

Giving birth to my great-grandmother was a hazardous and arduous experience for Beth Williams, as it was for any mother at that time. Families were counted by two numbers; those children that survived and those lost to miscarriages, stillbirths or death in infancy. There was no pain relief available. The midwife tied a strip of material to the end of the bed and instructed Beth to pull on it. Beth felt the agony of every tightening contraction. And when, finally, she felt the warmth of her daughter on her breast, the elation of motherhood was dampened with concerns that the child would not survive the summer. By one count my great-grandmother was the third of Thomas and Beth's children, fourth by another. The previous year their first daughter, Elizabeth, had died at thirteen weeks. In memory of her, and after both her mother and grandmother, this new child was also named Elizabeth.

Thomas was not in St David's to welcome his daughter. In May he had left his farming business and travelled down to Cardiff, leaving his wife alone to her labour and the care of their two sons. The prospects of the coal and iron industries of Glamorgan were attracting men out of the rural areas and into the mines and associated trades. On the strength of its exports, Cardiff was growing into an affluent city, with large department stores, theatres, hotels and respectable villas built along tree-lined avenues. Thomas was one of many men eager to take advantage of its escalating wealth. Two of Thomas's sisters were already in Cardiff. For the elder of the two, close to 30, the likelihood of marriage was fading rapidly. With the migration of men to the city, there were dozens of young women living in St David's who had little possibility of finding a husband locally. By the time Thomas and Beth and the family were reunited in Cardiff, the younger sister was engaged. The elder sister would eventually return home to the kitchens of Clegyr Isaf and remain unmarried.

The allure of Cardiff, for whatever reason the Williams family were drawn there, was only part of the story. Ten months before Elizabeth was born, Ebenezer Williams, son of George Williams, and Beth's brother, had rocked the righteous community of St David's with scandal. Ebenezer had established himself as the local pharmacist and sold insurance for the Farmers and General Life and Fire Insurance Company. He owned three cottages and a farm and had invested in shipping. Next to Old Cross, he had erected a heavy-set Georgian property with a wide shop front of three church windows, which overshadowed its old-fashioned neighbour. In August 1854, Ebenezer's enterprise failed. He filed for bankruptcy, his debts amounting to £11,000. Such an admission was a devastating disgrace for a very self-respecting Christian citizen at the heart of the community and a man dedicated to improving education in the town. That he should let his affairs reach such a nadir reflected not only on himself but the whole family.

Ironically, Ebenezer's predicament centred on the very property that had brought the family to St David's in the first place – the ruin of Treginnis Uchaf. In 1832, George Williams had loaned £1,800 to one John Roberts against this farmhouse, the dwelling having been rebuilt soon after the fire. Roberts had since died, as had his daughter, tragically killed through falling into 'a tub of boiling wort'.[2] When George Williams also passed away, Roberts's grandson refused to repay the mortgage. Ebenezer, unwisely, chased the case through the courts for sixteen years until bankruptcy forced defeat upon him.

The 6 September 1854 edition of the *Haverfordwest & Milford Haven Telegraph* tactfully announced that the 'very excellent stock and business of Mr. Ebenezer Williams, of St. David's, who is retiring therefrom' were up for sale. The store was, the paper noted, 'the only one of the kind in the place' and the inventory worth around £500. 'Druggists, grocers, oil and colourmen [vendors of paint], and fancy stationers' were invited to buy. In October, crops and implements from Ebenezer's farm were up for grabs. His shares in shipping were sold off. The house on Cross Square was emptied. Mahogany wardrobes, tables, sideboards, Kidderminster and Brussels carpets, four-poster and French beds, chiffoniers, chairs – the lot, all put on the market. A few months later, Ebenezer's property and land holdings also came under the auctioneer's hammer. Broken, Ebenezer died soon afterwards at the age of 44, and was buried in the grounds of the cathedral – beside his father and grandparents, who had brought the family out of its misfortune and into the wealth he had squandered.

It was perhaps no wonder that the Williams family began to look beyond their humiliation in St David's for untarnished reputations elsewhere. Their local prestige was at its lowest potency since the loss of Treginnis Uchaf. Cardiff, however, was evidently not a success. Before two years were over, Thomas and Beth had left Wales altogether and were headed for Liverpool.

The family, nevertheless, did leave behind a timely legacy in Cardiff. Thomas, with others, founded the Welsh-speaking Salem Presbyterian chapel close to the River Taff. The area had previously been the site of a medieval market, but was now being built on to provide housing for the new workers flooding into the city. Three years later, in 1859, a revival amongst the migrant community filled the chapel's wooden pews with converts. Regrettably, Thomas and Beth were not there to witness it.

The River Mersey was awash with great vessels under ballooning acres of canvas sail when the family arrived in Liverpool. The two older boys, John and George, hung over the ship's rail and plagued their father with questions about cargoes and destinations, while Elizabeth was held up by her mother to see the boats. In the distance, beyond a forest of ships' masts that obscured the quayside, the city rose out of a fog of smoke; a metropolis of chimneys and towers standing tall above closed ranks of houses. Thomas shepherded his sons onto a platform that floated alongside their ship and helped his wife and daughter across the iron bridge that brought the passengers to the top of the high dock walls and onto shore. A horse and carriage was hired and the new arrivals were driven a mile or so across the city to the more spacious environs of Everton.

The family found accommodation in a comfortable road close to parklands. The houses were generously sized, with gardens in which to grow vegetables. Here the claustrophobia and clatter of the city could be kept at bay. The choice was not incidental. From the mid-nineteenth century, Liverpool was home to around 20,000 Welsh migrants, mainly from north Wales, in a conurbation of less than half a million. Lacking a principal city of their own, Liverpool had become a de facto capital for the Welsh; Everton was, in part, a Welsh enclave. For Thomas and Beth, there was an added bonus that Liverpool was a stronghold of the Calvinistic Methodists. The community was centred around its chapels, where the new citizens found a familiar social order in which to maintain their church attendance, culture and language. Those already in employment were willing to help them find jobs in a city whose burgeoning shipping industry opened Europe's harbour mouth to the Atlantic Ocean.

In a curious historical coincidence, one of the Williams's neighbours was a tough Welsh boy aged around 16 by the name of John Rowlands, who arrived in Liverpool about the same year as Thomas and Beth. Master Rowlands had a reputation as a local ruffian. An illegitimate child, he had suffered the brutality of a workhouse before escaping and seeking a home with relatives. He was now in the care of a plain-speaking uncle down the road, who was trying to secure work for him. Young Elizabeth, at 2 and 3, would have been oblivious to his existence yet, extraordinarily, the life of John Rowlands would have a profound impact upon that of her future husband.

When the boy signed up on a ship to the United States two years later, John acquired both a new home country and a new name, Henry Morton Stanley. Much fêted as the man who located Dr David Livingstone, when the renowned London Missionary Society explorer went missing in central Africa, Stanley was the first European to map much of the Congo River, the region where Elizabeth's husband would commence his missionary career.

If Liverpool was a gold seam waiting to be mined, then application and ability were needed to prise nuggets out of its industry. Once again, as in Cardiff, it appears that Thomas Williams failed to establish himself. Thomas was first and foremost a farmer, like his father. He did not do well in the labyrinth of Liverpool's commercial colliery and spent no more than three years there. The family boarded a boat back to St David's, leaving the billowing sails and tall towers behind, their great adventure beyond the borders of Wales over.

Liverpool did, however, add another strand to the threads of my great-grandmother Elizabeth's life that God was slowly weaving together. In November 1830, Josiah Hughes, a bespectacled young missionary and one of the Welsh in Liverpool, arrived in Malacca, a British outpost on the coast of the Malay Peninsula. He was there under the auspices of the London Missionary Society (LMS) and was assigned work with the Muslim Malays. Hughes had wanted to go to India but the LMS refused his request. The Calvinistic Methodists of Liverpool took umbrage at the mission's high-handedness and when the mission denied another member of the chapel the opportunity to go to India, the Calvinistic Methodists of Liverpool withdrew their support of the LMS. In 1840 they founded their own 'Foreign Mission', the only noncon-formist Welsh denomination to do so. The impetus of this new venture was still alive when Thomas and Beth Williams walked into the Liverpool chapel. In the remote region of St David's this passion for overseas mission may well have been missed. In Liverpool there was no avoiding the zeal with which the committees of the Foreign Mission promoted service on the mission field through its appeals for workers and finance, and through the missionary hymns composed by its members. I doubt if Thomas and Beth would have anticipated then that their daughter would one day follow Josiah Hughes out to Asia as a missionary herself, but the thread was now woven into the fabric of their family life and was one she would weave into her own future.

Thomas and Beth returned home to St David's and to a cottage on Gospel Lane, the alleyway at the back of Old Cross where Elizabeth had been born five years before. The family took in a young woman, who acted as a house servant. Lettice Evans was an unmarried teenager, mother to an illegitimate baby, Ebenezer, whom the Williams appar-ently adopted. Thomas quietly resumed his position in the town's echelon of prominence. He found employment as a miller, later becoming a farm bailiff. He became a deacon at the Tabernacle Chapel and a long-serving teacher of the Sunday school, finding pleasure in passing on a love of music to his pupils. He and Beth had another child, Thomas, a late addition to the family. Tragically, this last son, like their first daughter, died before reaching adulthood, dying in 1879, aged 11.

There was, perhaps, a sense of relief in returning to the familiar traits and topography of the Treginnis Peninsula. There is no evidence that Thomas and Beth ventured beyond the borders of Wales, nor Pembrokeshire, again. But their brief, apparently unsuccessful, adventure evidently nurtured a desire to travel in their children. John, the eldest, returned to Liverpool. George became a sailor, venturing as far afield as Fuzhou on the east coast of China. Ebenezer, the adopted son, left St David's for Cardiff. And Elizabeth, as a single woman of 19, had no intention of being left at home. In 1874 she packed her possessions into a trunk and headed out of Wales, leaving behind the Celtic cross at the centre of St David's, which, unconcerned with change, continued to mark out her days as it had always done.

NOTES

[1] Patrick Henry, speech at the Second Virginia Convention at St. John's Church in Richmond, Virginia (23 March 1775); published as third person reference in W. Wirt, *Sketches of the Life and Character of Patrick Henry* (Philadelphia, PA: Webster, 1817), p. 120.

[2] Parish Register, quoted in Davies, *The Footsteps of Our Fathers*, p. 44. Wort is a liquid extracted in the brewing of beer.

3

The Smooth Waters of
St David's

'We none of us expect to be in smooth water all our days.'

Jane Austen, 1817[1]

When my great-grandmother decided to leave the perimeter of her protected upbringing in the superior houses of St David's, she grasped an impetus for change occurring in the lives of Welsh girls. Her formative years had rotated with clockwork conventionality about chapel, classroom and kitchen, but as she entered her teens there was a new momentum at work in society and it was this that carried her on a trajectory far beyond her beginnings.

At home, Elizabeth was the only daughter and therefore had no female siblings to share the household tasks allotted to her. The preparation of food for daily consumption, as gifts and for festivals governed the lives of women. Coming from a relatively wealthy family, Elizabeth's mother was able to provide her children with a richer diet than most mothers were able to. Relatives, having slaughtered a pig, offered cuts of the ribs and back chine to her father. Elizabeth's cousins arrived at the kitchen door with the joints in a basket, eagerly awaiting their penny reward for *hebrwng asgwrn*, 'sending a bone'. Lamb or beef could be bought and the neck of a fatted goose wrung for Christmas or New Year dinner. Women from the outlying villages brought cockles to the door to be served with fresh eggs or milk and chives. Home-made toffee, a luxury, could occasionally be bought from neighbours.

In general, though, the family's menus did not vary greatly. Elizabeth helped her mother to prepare a breakfast of bruised oatmeal cake and buttermilk with bread, butter and tea. Dinner, the most substantial meal of the day, was usually bacon and potatoes. Tea was taken at 4 o'clock with a bowl of *sucan*, a cold sour soup made from oat husks. Porridge with buttermilk was provided at supper. On the bakestone – a thin piece of stone hung on an iron frame over the open hearth – her mother produced oatcakes, *pancos* (oatmeal pancakes) spread with salted butter for birthdays, and little fruit turnovers. Once a week, loaves of bread were baked *bara dan cidl*, 'bread beneath the kettle'.

Oatmeal was the essential staple of much of the cooking Elizabeth's mother did. The cereal was kept in an oak chest in the bedroom above the kitchen, where the air was dry and warm and the oatmeal would not turn bitter. Her father and brothers carried the oatmeal home after it had been sifted and ground at her father's mill. Then every member of the family donned clean, white stockings and each in turn clambered into the chest and stamped and trampled the meal, until it was as tightly packed as possible. Stored like this, the meal would remain fresh and free from weevils until the next harvest.

Every recipe came with a set of precise instructions that Elizabeth was required to learn. Oatcake dough must be rotated periodically a quarter of the clock – those beneath the palm of the right hand clockwise, those on the left, anticlockwise – and then a pile of twelve cakes, layered with scoops of oatmeal, pressed again with palm and forearm to flatten them further. The use of a rolling pin was forbidden. The yellowing of a pinch of oatmeal on the bakestone meant the stone was hot enough. Finally, the cooked white oatcakes must be 'rested', balanced against the legs of an inverted three-legged stool by the fire.

Bread making brought more instructions. '*Peidiwch â boddi'r melinydd* . . . Don't drown the miller,' Elizabeth's mother would say as water was added to the flour. '*Gadael i'r toes ganu* . . . Let the dough sing,' when Elizabeth pummelled it too hard. Sometimes she was told to place the rising dough in the warmth of her bed once she had vacated it in the morning. Making the sour soup, *sucan*, was an art, not just a recipe. The roughly sifted husks of oatmeal were soaked, strained with a fine sieve and boiled in a cauldron until they formed a pale brown potage. '*Mae'r sucan yn ffrwtian, bois* . . . The *sucan* is spluttering, boys,' her mother sang, before watching Elizabeth carefully pour the mixture into tin pans. 'No cracks when it sets, Elizabeth, or you will marry an ugly man,' was a warning designed to teach Elizabeth culinary excellence. Perfect *sucan* needed to be as smooth as a pebble with the faintest sheen gently burnishing the surface. There was, Elizabeth quickly learned, a lot of pride at stake in a Welsh kitchen. Welsh teenage girls would often remake *sucan* for fear of scorn over their cooking prowess and loss of ground in the marriage stakes.

It seemed it had always been this way. Generations of girls in voluminous white pinafores watching their mothers, in cotton blouses, skirts and wool aprons, bake and cook, clean and launder, passing their skills and secrets on to their daughters. Each Welsh county had developed its own styles of housekeeping; every area proud of its distinctive ways of doing things. Beth Williams had no reason to believe that it would be any different for Elizabeth and, perhaps, if she had allowed herself to speculate, she may have expected me to be still preparing oatcakes the way the women of Pembrokeshire had always done.

Handing down from one generation to the next was not confined to the kitchen. The house provided its own testament to the practice. Comb-back chairs, three-legged stools, dark oak dressers and carved Bible boxes were kept within the extended family for years. Cross-stitch and wool samplers, one or two of them stitched no doubt with supervised neatness by Elizabeth, bedecked the walls with biblical maxims. Small ornaments, acquired from department stores in Cardiff and Liverpool, cluttered ledges and shelves. These decorations, however, were kept in shadow, the sun rarely allowed to get beyond the heavy curtains.

Elizabeth's education in pride in the kitchen and in the home did not restrict her from exploration of the lanes and open heathlands around St David's. Searching for bird nests was a local favourite pastime. In the spring there were as many as thirty nests to watch over as the drama of the hatching of eggs and first flutters of flight unfolded. Jackdaws had colonized the Bishop's Palace, filling the holes in the masonry with brushwood. Argumentative starlings had possession of the evergreens around Rock House, the five-bedroomed town house with servants' quarters that her widowed grandmother, Elizabeth Williams of Llys-y-frân, had owned. Hedge sparrows occupied the moor, where parasitical cuckoos usurped their nests, and blackcaps hid themselves away amongst the yellow gorse. On Ramsey Island, off the Treginnis Peninsula, were cormorants, kittiwakes and razorbills, and further out to sea, on the crags of the Bishops and Clerks, there were puffins. Elizabeth's older brother, George, was not averse to scaling the hazardous 300 foot cliffs of Allt Felyn Fawr on Ramsey Island – 'every little niche and ledge . . . occupied by some member of the feathered tribe . . . tier upon tier, the whole cliff side resembling rows of white waistcoated minstrels'[2] – to collect gulls' eggs, bringing them home for boiling or to sell the prettier ones to collectors.

Elizabeth's life at home and on the heathland was not vastly different from that of her mother and grandmothers, but the classroom offered a different opportunity. Wales had been scandalized by the publication of a government survey into education in 1847. *Brad y Llyfrau Gleision*, 'The Treachery of the Blue Books', stung the Welsh into reform of teaching standards, curricula and facilities. The reports slammed the educational, social and moral state of the nation. Schools were held in dark, damp barns, church halls or private homes. Teachers were unqualified and poorly paid. The living conditions of the lower classes were criticized for the scarcity of toilets, for the lack of bed linen on cupboard beds that remained closed from dawn to dusk, for their deprived two-roomed homes and their 'particularly dirty'[3] habits. The use of the Welsh language and religious nonconformity were blamed for the immoral state of the nation and, more specifically, of its women.

Ralph Robert Wheeler Lingen, the 'most formidable and least sympathetic of the commissioners',[4] chastised the St David's region with his observations, 'It is miserably provided with schools, and is in other respects much neglected.'[5] The seven day schools in St David's, run by churches, chapels or privately, lacked sufficient furniture, and each had only one teacher, none of whom had formal training. Among their ranks were a farmer, a joiner, a labourer and a sailor.

In the years before Elizabeth was born, the religious and social reformers of Wales set about transforming the country's educational system, bent on proving that the nation was not as degraded and immoral as the Blue Books had testified. The desire to have an illegitimacy rate no worse than England's became a national obsession. New schools were built. English was promoted as the panacea to raise living standards. The curriculum for girls was paid particular attention, focusing initially on academic rather than domestic studies. My great-grandmother was amongst the first generation of girls profitably placed to benefit from the reforms. Beyond primary education, St David's had a grammar school at the cathedral, and two private secondary schools, one specifically for girls. Elizabeth took full advantage of the opportunity and studied until the age of 16. She had ambitions to be usefully employed outside the farming community, and avoid the routine path into the graft of domestic service.

The third influential setting of my great-grandmother's upbringing, the chapel, was something of a mixed blessing for a girl. Tabernacle Chapel was run by a male hierarchy of dark-suited ministers and elders. The role of women was articulated from the pulpit and reinforced by the chapel's practices. But these men were also anxious to provide education for the town's female population, basing lessons around the reading of Bible passages and hymn singing. Elizabeth attended the largest Sunday school in the town. For two hours each week she learned to read, sitting amongst the rows of children and adults on rough wooden benches in the sizeable hall of the Tabernacle Chapel. Later, she would have joined three dozen and more men and women as a teacher. In addition there were regular meetings, entertainment and outings organized specifically for women by the chapel leadership; occasions which provided opportunities for my great-grandmother to build confidence in her abilities.

Sunday attendance of chapel was integral to family life. Elizabeth's everyday wear was set aside for the formality of (what is now considered to be) Welsh national costume. Her pinafore dress was replaced with a full skirt and dark woollen bedgown, with its waistcoat front, short sleeves and distinctive tail. Knitted stockings, purchased from itinerant pedlars who carried their wares on a 'stocking horse', were hooked around one of her toes, and her feet slipped into alder wood clogs with leather uppers. On colder days she draped a blue cloak around her shoulders, and over this the all-important shawl of colourful cotton or, on special occasions, paisley patterned silk. Finally, there was the donning of her distinctive conical, wide-brimmed silk hat. But fashions were changing and teenage girls were becoming independent enough to resist the styles of their mothers and leave their dark, attractive hair on view before the chapel service started.

Tabernacle Chapel had become something of a Williams's family enterprise. Elizabeth's grandfathers had been responsible for the chapel's construction. Her father was a deacon, as was one of her uncles. And the incumbent minister was George Williams, her mother's older brother, who, having married the minister's daughter, had succeeded his father-in-law. Despite his stern Sunday countenance, deep-set dark eyes and solemn expression, Elizabeth had nothing to fear from Uncle George. I suspect that George, a widower, had a soft spot for his niece as a companion to his only child, Mary Anne.

I have no letters that relate exactly when my great-grandmother found a personal faith in God. Perhaps it was as a young girl while learning Bible stories from her mother, or from her father's love of hymn singing, possibly through listening to her uncle's sermons, or maybe once she emerged into the buoyancy of her teenage years. It is clear, however, that it was not in any way simply acquiescence to family expectation. Her life and poignant death demonstrate the profound depth of her commitment to Christ.

As Elizabeth approached her twenties it must have seemed as though the world had no boundaries. There were letters from Liverpool from her brother John, and news from George sent from ports all along the route to China and back. Ebenezer, though four years younger than she was, was off to Cardiff. Elizabeth was well educated in English and not content to remain in the remote recess of south-west Wales. St David's held little attraction for her. Like her aunts, she knew the prospects for marriage were slim with so few eligible men left in the district. Locally there were meagre work prospects for an intelligent young woman. She would train as a nurse, a profession whose growing status matched her own aspirations. She would go to London.

NOTES

[1] Jane Austen, *Persuasion* (London: John Murray, first published 1817, dated 1818), ch. 8.

[2] H. Evans, *Twr-y-felin: History and Guide to St David's* (St David's, Twr-y-Felin Hotel: private publication, 2nd edn, 1923), p. 112.

[3] *Reports of the Commissioners of Inquiry into the State of Education in Wales: Part 1: Carmarthen, Glamorgan and Pembroke* (London: Her Majesty's Stationery Office, 1847), p. 20. Used with permission: LLGC: The National Library of Wales.

[4] D.W. Howell, ed., *Pembrokeshire County History, Volume IV: Modern Pembrokeshire 1815–1874* (Haverfordwest: The Pembrokeshire Historical Society, 1993), p. 393. Used with permission: Pembrokeshire County History Trust.

[5] *Reports of the Commissioners of Inquiry*, p. 394.

4

London – Fulfilment of Ambition

'The want of remunerative occupations suitable for gentlewomen is, in these days, painfully felt and universally acknowledged ... But it appears that there is one department of activity peculiarly their own, which they have hitherto failed to make the vantage-ground it might become. We refer to nursing.'

Charlotte Haddon, 1871[1]

London, when Elizabeth arrived in 1874, was a maelstrom of encounters into which she was plunged with little preparation. Paddington Station, a glazed tunnel of immense wrought-iron arches, housed the terminus of 'God's Wonderful Railway' – the Great Western Railway, and seemed large enough to shelter any one of Wales's villages. Beyond the close ranks of offices that lined the platform lay the foreign streets of the capital of the British Empire. It was a city that commanded the affairs of the world while grappling with the challenges of mass migration into its overcrowded neighbourhoods. Within the sixty-three years of Queen Victoria's reign, the city tripled its population, absorbing more and more citizens, who lived 'chameleon-like, upon the air'.[2] The coffers of the Bank of England were filled with more gold than those of any other nation and yet, in its markets, girls of 8 and 9 in thin cotton dresses sold four bunches of watercress for a penny.

Elizabeth was suddenly surrounded by the colossal edifices of newly built hotels, museums and educational establishments; architectural adventures in colour and style which quickly lost their fresh façades beneath layers of smoke and grime. In wretched contrast, great portions of the population were crammed into 'rookeries'; slums strained to the limit, some literally awash with effluent and the debris of a poverty-stricken existence. Crime was rife. The nation that policed the world chased child thieves and pickpockets, 'fluttering in rags and the most motley attire',[3] from Shoreditch to St Giles and Westminster to Whitechapel. The city was a miscellany of beggars and burglars, cadgers and costermongers, prostitutes and gamblers, swag-shop owners and swindlers, all crammed into the cracks and crevices between the broad avenues of the rich and influential.

London had benefited from a distinctive, but unobtrusive, Welsh presence for two centuries. Farmers from Wales had grazed their cattle in its meadows, and their daughters sold milk on its streets. As the city expanded, claiming pastureland for building, these enterprises were transformed first into 'Cow Keeper' shops and then into dairies. Itinerant hosiers, like the ones that sold Elizabeth's mother stockings in St David's, found permanent niches in London and built up drapery businesses. And there were many others who joined them, bringing skilled trades and professional acumen to the capital; carpenters and masons, painters and French polishers, schoolmasters and surveyors. By the time Elizabeth arrived, Welsh chapels and churches, a natural place for her to find friendship and support, had begun to proliferate, reflecting a growing respectability and wealth. The Welsh in London were, however, scattered like seeds in a field; unlike Liverpool, there was no particular neighbourhood they made their own.

I know very little about what happened to Elizabeth in the five years between leaving St David's and arriving at the doors of London's University College Hospital in 1879, where she was about to start two years' nursing training with the All Saints' Sisters of the Poor. There is just one letter from an uncle to her and another written by a cousin many years later that provide small clues. Initially she trained as a children's nurse, working in a London hospital. There was time spent in Ramsgate, Kent, chaperoned by a spinster, Miss May. But in spring 1876 she was back in St David's. It is not difficult to believe that she needed to get her breath back, tread the familiar paths of Pembrokeshire, and take stock of her first experience of London.

When Elizabeth finally arrived at the steps of the south entrance of University College Hospital, standing beneath the gas lamp and looking beyond the narrow doorway, she had, no doubt, a few nerves to settle. In the journey of her life the short walk of a few hundred yards from the Georgian flat-fronted brick terraces where she lodged had taken minutes. Nevertheless, this event represented a significant waymark in the fulfilment of her teenage ambitions, and brought the man she would marry into her path.

University College Hospital was, then, a very different structure to the red-brick elaboration of the cruciform building that now occupies the site on London's Gower Street. Surrounded by plain iron railings, the grey stucco structure was solidly rectangular, rising to four floors and topped with tall chimneys. It was a relatively plain building, deliberately erected with economy in mind. The main façade still carried in bold lettering the original name, the 'North London Hospital', and it looked across Gower Street to the sparse gardens and ostentatious portico of the hospital's founding institution, University College. The hospital had been built as a practical training facility for the university's medical students, primarily serving the poor who could not afford private treatment.

On her first day at the hospital, Elizabeth smoothed down her dress in the convenient reflection of a window, mounted the four stone steps to the hospital doors, and walked as quickly and as silently as she could down the long corridor to her ward, ready for a ten-hour shift working side by side with the All Saints' nurses. She was dressed in her own clothes, carefully chosen for her probation. It would be three months before she would be allowed to wear a uniform; a full-length, black gown protected by a white, starched apron. She would also be given a stiff-winged coif, a close fitting cap, designed to keep her hair brushed back so that stray locks would not fall over her forehead. Nurses must be 'neatly and quietly dressed'[4] her manual informed her, a code calculated to keep her demeanour, like her hair, precisely in place. 'Ornaments' were to be avoided, but she was advised to carry a well-stocked pincushion and scissors suspended from her apron waistband. She must obtain 'quiet boots without trimming';[5] high-heeled boots, which 'cannot but be noisy',[6] were prohibited.

The All Saints' sisterhood had taken control of the nursing at the hospital in April 1862, relieving the matron, a Miss Robottom, and her staff of their duties. The hospital had originally housed 130 beds but facilities had increased to 200 beds with an extension upwards to include a fourth floor. For their services, the sisterhood received £1,000 per annum and surrendered any rights to influence the religious sentiments of the patients 'by word or deed, or by the distribution or withholding of books'.[7] This condition was not without good reason as far as their employers were concerned. The sister-hood, founded in 1851, was one of a growing number of high church vocational Anglican orders, modelled on women's groups in Europe and viewed with Victorian suspicion. Such societies were, their critics alleged, vehicles for feminism, Roman Catholicism in uniform, indulging in financial deception and cruelty to members, or run by power-drunk, sadistic mothers superior. All Saints', for their part, ignored the denigration and had become a highly efficient nursing organization, considered to be one of the best in England. They drew 'Women of Superior Class'[8] into their ranks to pursue the 'love of Christ, the end and aim of all their works, prayers and words'.[9] With deliberate dexterity they promoted their practical nursing skills amongst the poor, while privately developing an inner spiritual life; surprisingly, perhaps, esteeming the former as more imperative than the latter.

The wedding of a high Anglican sisterhood to so-called 'Godless' University College was a strange marriage, owing more to pragmatism than principle.[10] The college had been founded in 1826 to provide a university education for medical students of moderate means. Students were accepted regardless of religion, race or political persuasion. This non-sectarian stance was a deliberately devised alternative to the Anglican bias of Oxford and Cambridge. The Hospital Committee wondered whether it was wise to hand the nursing over to an organization 'holding peculiar religious views'.[11] Ironically, the College Council, more concerned with the atrocious state of the nursing at the hospital, were less particular and invited All Saints' onto its territory.

'The place was a proper shambles when All Saints' arrived,' Elizabeth was told. 'Sister Caroline Mary was here. She said that the nurses were drinking the patients' medicines. One of them had to be dismissed for drunkenness. The last matron apparently put in a request for stronger beer to be delivered to her table!'

'We all know that the patients take things home but, can you believe it, a nurse was caught stealing two mattresses, a set of fire irons and a table! Another was selling morphia to the patients and a third in court for pawning the sheets.'

'And when a night nurse actually stole the boots of one of the doctors, can you imagine the scandal!'

The invitation to the All Saints' sisterhood was in part due to Sir William Jenner, discoverer of the difference between typhus and typhoid and an eminent physician at the hospital. One evening Jenner had come across a night porter cooking a chicken on the ward fire and drinking hot brandy at the invitation of the nurses. The ward was untidy, dirty and the patients utterly neglected. Too many of the old nurses or 'Gamps', as Dickens had characterized them in the disreputable and alcoholic umbrella-carrying Sairey Gamp,[12] were women of 'inadequate skill, coarse manners, low character, and bibulous tendencies',[13] 'too old, too weak, too drunken, too dirty, too stolid or too bad to do anything else'.[14]

Jenner had decided that action was needed. Following the Crimean War, advanced by the formidable influence of Florence Nightingale and others, attitudes to nursing were changing rapidly. Semi- or un-skilled older women with no other way of earning money were no longer considered up to the task. Ward staff capable of reading and writing were needed. New surgery techniques required more skill from surgeons, dressers and nurses. Nursing was becoming a laudable profession, attracting the interest of single middle class girls with an education, such as Elizabeth. In 1860, Jenner asked All Saints' to provide two nurses, and within two years the old shambolic order had been deposited outside the hospital doors, swept away by the cleanliness, efficiency and high moral standing of the newcomers. God and cleanliness were, as far as the sisterhood were concerned, intimately related, a principle Elizabeth was already well versed in.

There remains the curious question of how my great-grandmother found herself a probationary member of an Anglican order, which required her to be a member of the Church of England and to have the recommendation of a clergyman. The family were, after all, at home in Welsh-speaking nonconformist circles. Oddly, while the cathedral congregation felt the loss of members to the Methodists keenly, the Calvinistic Methodists of St David's retained an affection for the old church. After their 9 o'clock Sunday service, groups of them would file down the hill and stand in the spaces between the cathedral's north and south doors, listening to the music and prayers of the Anglican 10 o'clock service.

Whatever the process by which Elizabeth made her change from Calvinistic Methodist chapel to Anglican cloisters, she was obviously ecumenical in outlook, for within a few years she had exited the wide gates of the Church of England and become a Baptist.

Elizabeth, apparently, had no plans to become a novice, but in joining the order she accepted the obligations of a religious life. Prayer bracketed the working day. She was instructed to rise at seven, breakfast at 7:30 and be at prayer by eight. Supper, the fourth meal of the day, was followed by prayers at 9:30 p.m. After devotions she was required to retire quietly to her room and be in bed with the gas lamp extinguished by 10:30. Lighting candles to catch a few more minutes for herself was forbidden. Even on the wards, the daily routines of prayer were not forgotten. The Oratory, a room on the top floor of the hospital, was set aside for the nurses to say the lesser hours and vespers, as work permitted.

Three months after starting her training, Elizabeth was upgraded to assistant nurse and received a small wage, in the region of £20 per year; a sum supplemented by full board, washing facilities and the cost of medical help. It was a better salary than that of a maid or cook in one of the larger houses, but it did not compare with the £30 or more that the mistress of the house might spend on dresses each year. She was also given an outdoor uniform, which she must wear at all times outside of the hospital. This was rarely more than the short walk to and from her lodgings. If she wanted to go further afield, she must get permission from the sister superior. Initially permitted no more than two hours' absence, she must return by 8 p.m. It was another five months before she received a pass entitling her to stay out from six till ten, once a week.

Whatever priorities my great-grandmother had as she entered the doors of University College, her obedience to the rules of her order was quickly put to the test. Amongst the strict codes of conduct, which were more severe than those laid down in other institutions opening their doors to women, the rules governing relationships with eligible men were particularly troublesome. Husband hunting was disapproved of and, when occasion demanded, vehemently condemned – which made it difficult for Elizabeth when Herbert Dixon walked on to the ward, a good-looking young man with a determined look in his eyes. With a polite tip of his head he addressed her.

'Miss Williams.'

'Mr Dixon?'

It did not take long for Herbert to engage Elizabeth in conversation. Time, after all, was limited. He was at the hospital for just one year, training as a doctor, he explained. Then he was going overseas as a missionary. Visits to Britain would be few. Perhaps they could meet?

NOTES

[1] C. Haddon, 'Nursing as a Profession for Ladies', *St Paul's Monthly Magazine*, August 1871, p. 458.

[2] H. Mayhew, *London Labour and the London Poor: Vol. 3, The London Street-Folk; comprising, Street sellers. Street buyers. Street finders. Street performers. Street artizans. Street labourers* (London: Griffin, Bohn, and Company, 1861), p. 308.

3 H. Mayhew, *London Labour and the London Poor: Vol. 4, Those that will not work; comprising, Prostitutes. Thieves. Swindlers. Beggars* (London: Griffin, Bohn, and Company, 1862), p. 273.

4 E.J. Domville, *A Manual for Hospital Nurses* (London: J & A Churchill, 1875), p. 1.

5 Regulation of The Society of All Saints' Sisters of the Poor, 1862. Used with permission: All Saints' Sisters of the Poor.

6 E.J. Domville, *A Manual for Hospital Nurses*, p. 2.

7 University College Hospital General Committee minutes, 1857–1866, April 1862, quoted in S.W.F. Holloway, 'The All Saints' Sisterhood at University College Hospital, 1862–99', *Medical History*, April 1959, p. 149.

8 Provision of The Society of All Saints' Sisters of the Poor, 1862.

9 Provision of The Society of All Saints' Sisters of the Poor, 1859.

10 The description of University College as 'Godless' reflects the reaction of the Anglican Church to the university's foundation on non-sectarian principles. The founding of the college was supported by nonconformist Christians, who wanted the opportunity of university education for their sons.

11 University College Hospital General Committee minutes, 1857–1866, April 1862, quoted in S.W.F. Holloway, *Medical History*, p. 148.

12 Charles Dickens, *Life and Adventures of Martin Chuzzlewit* (London: Chapman and Hall, 1844).

13 F.J.C. Hearnshaw, *The Centenary History of King's College London, 1828–1928* (London: Harrap, 1929), p. 232. Used with permission: S. Wall.

14 Florence Nightingale, *Report of the Committee Appointed to Consider the Cubic Space of Metropolitan Workhouses* (London: Her Majesty's Stationery Office, 1867), p. 64.

5

Mr Dixon – My Great-Grandfather

'A good education is a fortune a child can never spend.'
Andrew Reed, 1787–1862[1]

SECOND APPLICATION—JANUARY ELECTION, 1866.

To the Governors and Subscribers of the

LONDON ORPHAN ASYLUM,

CLAPTON.

The Favour of your Vote and Interest is most respectfully solicited on behalf of

HERBERT DIXON,

AGED NINE YEARS,

Whose Father was a Flour Factor, and died of consumption in 1863, leaving a Widow and Five Children unprovided for, three of whom are now dependent on the Mother.

The case is strongly recommended by the following:

Rev. T. D. Lamb, West Hackney.	Messrs. Harris Brothers, 8, Leadenhall Street.
Dr. Metcalfe, Portland Place, Clapton.	* Mr. Bowman, 17, Cambridge Terrace, Kingsland.
Revd. Thornhill, Esq., Wickham Place, Clapton.	Wm. Medland, Esq., Dunstable, Beds.
M. B. Metcalfe, Esq. Wickham Place, Clapton.	

*Proxies will be thankfully received by those marked * and also by the Mother, Stoke Newington Common.*

Alongside the sepia Victorian photographs, yellowing letters and brown newspaper cuttings in the family's old, black tin box there is a small buff-coloured card. Measuring a few centimetres high and wide, it is a printed plea to the 'Governors and Subscribers of the London Orphan Asylum', the second application for admission of a child to an orphanage in Clapton, east London, dated January 1866. At the bottom of the card is a list of names – among them the Reverend T.D. Lamb of West Hackney, Robert Thornhill, a flour merchant, and William Medland, a solicitor from Dunstable – all sponsors of this appeal. At the centre of the card in large lettering is the name of the child for whom votes are 'most respectively solicited': Herbert Dixon, my great-grandfather, aged 9.

This was such a sad discovery. On first appearance I found it shocking that a member of my family had been reduced to such straits. But, as I explored the circumstances and their consequences, I can see that it was the saving of this young man from a desperate situation in more ways than one. If Elizabeth's family in St David's was rising on a tide of business acumen and wealth, then the fortunes of my great-grandfather's family were the very opposite. Left at a very low ebb due to the death of his father, Benjamin Dixon, in 1863, Herbert, his four brothers, and Emily, their mother, were quickly stranded on the brink of poverty.

When Benjamin began to cough up blood, Herbert's mother must have been heartbroken. Emily would have been in little doubt that her husband was headed for the grave. Consumption (now known as tuberculosis) was rife in Victorian England, claiming the lives of one in eight of her citizens. The 'captain of all these men of death',[2] as Bunyan described the disease, was a killer with little regret for its fevered victims. Emily was bequeathed an inadequate pension and a fragile future. Despite her best efforts, their financial situation worsened until her most terrible fears were realized. It was impossible to keep the family together. One of her children would have to be taken into care. Arthur and Edwin, the eldest, were already old enough to find work. Charles would only be in school for another year, perhaps two, before he could find a job. Oliver, the youngest at 6, was too young to let go. I cannot imagine her pain, or my great-grandfather's confusion, as she tearfully took Herbert on one side and explained that, for the sake of them all, he was going away.

Nevertheless, Emily was more fortunate than many widows, who were simply condemned to the unforgiving regime of the workhouse. Benjamin had done well enough for himself. Moving from the family home in rural Essex, he established himself in his thirties as a flour merchant in the select residential area of Stoke Newington, still sufficiently untouched by London to be a quiet village of around seven hundred houses. A bachelor till the late age of 37, he met and, in 1850, married Emily Reynolds, a woman from Birmingham who was eleven years younger than himself.

The couple's first home was close to London's docklands, where tall chimneys choked the maritime streets with dark smoke, labourers in dirty shirts and greasy jackets lived in low-grade lodgings, and where unemployment was endemic. It was not to Benjamin and Emily's liking and, with a growing family, they found a better home on the more pleasant inclines of Stamford Hill, above Stoke Newington. The house belonged to a brewery and stood in a neighbourhood of folk betwixt and between, comfortably placed, but by no means rich. It was here that Herbert was born, their fourth son. Benjamin's business prospered, allowing him to employ three men and two boys. Consumption, however, was not confined to the overcrowded rookeries of London. Nor was it particular whether its dead were prosperous or poor. In February 1863, Benjamin was buried among the grey graves at Abney Park Cemetery, a rambling graveyard for nonconformist believers, quarter of a mile from his first home in Stoke Newington.

Emily's second application to the London Orphan Asylum was successful. My great-grandfather was plucked from the rough companionship of his brothers and the familiarity of home. He found himself surrounded by bewildering hordes of boys – close to three hundred of them, all uniformly dressed in dark blue jackets, waistcoats and trousers, marshalled by six young schoolmasters. There were girls too. The orphanage housed 150 schoolgirls, clad in brown merino sheep wool dresses protected by an obligatory holland pinafore. It is doubtful that Herbert, whether indifferent or interested, was ever allowed much contact with them. There was vigilant segregation of the sexes. Separate classrooms, dining halls, play areas and teachers – masters for the boys, governesses for the girls – kept them apart. Chapel was possibly the only time the genders were ever considered safe together, and even then they were seated on opposite sides of the church.

Herbert's hair was trimmed to a smart length, fortunately not with the 'rigorous discipline of scissors'[3] enforced at other institutions, and he was told to get into his uniform. His dormitory was a barrack-like first floor room, 100 feet long with large windows, the beds pushed together along two sides of a central partition. It was orderly, but crowded. There were around thirty boys his age sharing the space with dozens of teenagers and children as young as 7. As I visualize my great-grandfather, a small boy living out this unexpected life, largely away from his family, I have no doubt that it was here that he developed a compassion for the poor and the sick. It was also here that God, in his love and wisdom, taught him the resilience and courage he displayed in later life.

The London Orphan Asylum was the inspiration of the Reverend Doctor Andrew Reed, a Congregational minister with a penchant for founding institutions for the unfortunate,[4] who believed that the 'widow and orphan have an undisputed claim to our benevolence'.[5] His contemporaries described him as tall and handsome, with a melodious voice and forceful manner. Despite his humble station as a nonconformist minister, he mixed with the influential and charmed or bullied his way into their purses. The Duke of Wellington, no mean man himself, persuaded to attend a fundraising dinner, described Reed as 'that great man, whose wishes are to me law, and, whose entreaties I felt as a command it was impossible to resist'.[6] Reed persuaded Princess Victoria's father to chair one of the institution's festival dinners in 1815. He invited another of the king's sons to lay the foundation stone (something of a PR disaster as the distinguished party fell into the hole for the foundations when the platform collapsed), and a third to open the finished building in 1825. When he died, a few months before Herbert's father, Reed's legacy was carved in a memorial in the orphanage that depicted him bending over three children, offering a plate of bread with one hand and a Bible with the other. Such was his talent for extracting cash from the moneyed that in his lifetime Reed raised £1,043,566 for his charities.

Among the many supporters of the London Orphan Asylum encouraged to generosity by Reed was an architect, James Edmeston. Edmeston was a literary man, publishing poems and over two thousand hymns. One of these hymns,

'Lead us, heavenly Father, lead us', he dedicated to the children at the orphanage. The words are a poignant reminder of the plight of the children Reed wanted to help and of the faith in a provider God that the foundation taught my great-grandfather. Herbert, after all, no longer had a father to help him:

> Lead us, heavenly Father, lead us,
> O'er the world's tempestuous sea;
> Guard us, guide us, keep us, feed us,
> For we have no help but Thee;
> Yet possessing every blessing,
> If our God our Father be.[7]

At the time of my great-grandfather's arrival, the institution had already provided an education for over two and a half thousand children. The orphanage was not solely for children who had lost both parents, nor did it cater for the hapless poor. The children were carefully selected; the offspring of beleaguered families 'in respectable circumstances'.[8] Emily provided proof that her husband had died, a certificate of her marriage and evidence of Herbert's state of good health. Questions were asked to ascertain that Benjamin had been 'of Professional men, of Principals engaged in Agriculture, Manufacture, Commerce or Trade, or of Mercantile or other Clerks, and of those in like position'.[9] This, however, was no more than the introduction to an intricate process of 'education by election'.[10] Entry into the asylum was by no means straightforward. Competition for places was keen. Emily drew on what finances she had, the remains of her husband's goodwill and her own persistence to secure Herbert a place. Cards, like the one I have, soliciting votes for election to the school, needed to be printed and distributed in their hundreds. Thousands of votes must be secured from subscribers to the orphanage. Elections were held in January and July when places were given to the requisite numbers of boys and girls at the head of the polling lists. The saving grace in the system was that votes could be carried forward from one election to the next, giving those who had made a previous application an advantage over new candidates.[11]

To outward appearances, the London Orphan Asylum was a majestic building, built on three sides of a quadrangle set behind gardens of small shrubs in eight acres of land. At the crest of the horseshoe drive stood the centrepiece, a two-storey high chapel and its colonnades, fronted by four robust Doric columns and a doorway that looked at first glance to have been built for giants. In reality, the stately façade obscured problems that were becoming obvious as Herbert entered the institution's wrought-iron gates. What had once been a pleasant semi-rural site was now trapped amongst unhealthy factories and housing. The dormitories were overfull; the beds squeezed to no more than 18 inches apart. Lavatory and washing facilities were inadequate for around four hundred and fifty pupils, 15 staff members, 18 female servants, a matron and a seamstress. In the autumn of 1866, typhoid took a devastating hold and 200 children fell ill; fifteen of my great-grandfather's companions died. Plans were made to relocate to a thirty-six acre site in Watford, but Herbert, at 14, left the ailing orphanage before these were realized.

It was Herbert's good fortune, nevertheless, to be given a quality education. For five and a half days each week he sat in the huge hall beneath his dormitory, his class hidden from others by green baize curtains hung on brass rods. One of the schoolmasters surveyed the proceedings from a raised dais at the far end of the hall, while the older boys taught him to read and write and instructed him in what they knew of arithmetic, history and geography. He was also schooled in the regimes of French and Latin declensions and grappled with the perplexities of algebra and geometry; new subjects on the curriculum. His first lesson of the day commenced around 6:30 before breakfast, bowls of oatmeal boiled in half a pint of milk and bread 'never less than two days old',[12] and attendance at chapel. When classes finished ten hours later, there was another round of chapel services, followed by supper and bed.

The asylum vowed 'to fix the habits of industry and frugality; to train [its pupils] in the paths of religion and virtue'.[13] Industry came through the maintenance and mending tasks the children were expected to perform. Frugality was learned in the dining hall, where meals were eaten in silence after eight boys had sung grace in the corridor between the boys' and girls' rooms. Broth and suet pudding were the regular diet; meat being available only four days a week and green vegetables an occasional extravagance. Religion was administered in the twice daily attendance of chapel. Virtue was handed out in a currency system.

Herbert earned coins for 'minor virtues':[14] cleanliness, kindness, neatness, perseverance and punctuality. The concept of cleanliness, however, left something to be desired by modern standards. A table printed in 1839 laid out the following provisions:

- Children to wash hands and faces when get up and before going to bed.
- Children to wash necks twice a week.
- Feet to be washed once a week and 'their persons made thoroughly clean'.[15]

Major virtues such as contentment, honesty and patience were rewarded with medals hung on pale blue ribbons and a name on the master's roll of honour. The list of minor offences, for which monetary fines must be paid, was depressingly longer than either of those for minor and major virtues. The breaking of *any* of the Ten Commandments was a sure way to receive the rod and a diet of bread and water, though the children would have been hard pressed to violate some of them!

I have no idea what Master Herbert Dixon and his classmates, Arthur Andrews, Henry Wegforth and Thomas Tow, got up to in their idle moments. While it is tempting to hope that he was a model pupil, I suspect my great-grandfather's tendency to hot-headedness got the better of him and he was on occasions called to the office of the headmaster to learn the orphanage's objectives the hard way.

London Orphan Asylum was also the place where Herbert first felt the call to become a missionary. Reed himself had hoped to join the London Missionary Society's work in China but was unable to go. There were regular missionary addresses at the school, and collections for missionaries living at the very tip of South America in the exotic-sounding province of Patagonia. From then on, Herbert later said, 'missionary subjects were continually on his mind, and, reading various accounts, from time to time, of the deplorable ignorance of the heathen, he resolved that, if God permitted him, he would go and endeavour to enlighten them'.[16]

When Herbert left the institution, he no doubt followed many of the boys into employment in businesses owned by members of the orphanage board before he was able to pursue his calling to the mission field.[17] By the time Herbert, in his early twenties, met Elizabeth on the wards of University College Hospital, he was alone in the world again. All his brothers had gone to make a living in South Africa. Two years earlier, his mother had died aged 53. He had buried Emily alongside his father in Abney Park Cemetery. As he walked away from the grave, perhaps he stopped for a few moments to read the inscription on the towering red granite obelisk that stands close to the entrance gates, 'He that abideth in me, and I in him, the same bringeth forth much fruit'.[18] The monument is a final memorial to Andrew Reed, whose vision established my great-grandfather in his love for God, a compassion for those less fortunate than himself, and his longing to bring others to Christ.

In the words of Edmeston's orphanage hymn, the seas that lay ahead of my great-grandfather were tempestuous ones. The challenges that Herbert would face in obedience to God's call were ones that most of us would shy away from. I have no doubt that the petitions and promises of this hymn became his lifelong prayer.

NOTES

[1] Attributed to Andrew Reed or possibly his maternal grandfather, private correspondence with M. Fitzgerald, Reed's

School, Cobham, Surrey, 4 October 2010. Used with permission: Reed's School.

2 John Bunyan, *The Life and Death of Mr. Badman, Presented to the World in a Familiar Dialogue between Mr. Wiseman, and Mr. Attentive* (London: Nathaniel Ponder, 1680), ch. 18.

3 E. Yates, *Illustrated Times*, 1858, quoted in P. Horton, *The London Orphan Asylum (Clapton 1825–1871): Notes for a History* (unpublished manuscript, Hackney Archives, London, ca. 1960–1968). Used with permission: Reed's School.

4 Reed founded the Infant Orphan Asylum, later called the Royal Wanstead School, in 1827; the Asylum for Fatherless Children, later established in Purley and called Reedham School, in 1844; the Asylum for Idiots, later the Royal Earlswood Hospital, Redhill, in 1847; and the Royal Hospital for Incurables, Putney, in 1854. The London Orphan Asylum was later renamed Reed's School, an independent school for day and boarding pupils located in Cobham, Surrey.

5 A. Reed, 27 July 1815, quoted in *Reed's School, Cobham: The Archive of the Secretary to the Governors, 1814–1988* http://www.exploringsurreyspast.org.uk/GetRecord/SHCOL_3719_(PART1OF2) (accessed 6 February 2012). Used with permission: Reed's School.

6 Duke of Wellington, A. Reed and C. Reed, *Memoirs of the Life and Philanthropic Labours of Andrew Reed D.D.* (London: Strahan and Co., 1863), p. 495.

7 James Edmeston (1791–1867), 'Lead us, heavenly Father, lead us', *Sacred Lyrics, Second Set* (London: Holdsworth, 1821), p. 31.

8 London Orphan Asylum regulation, quoted in N. Alvey, *Education by Election: Reed's School, Clapton and Watford* (St Albans: St Albans and Hertfordshire Architectural and Archaeological

Society, 1990), p. 2. Used with permission: N. Alvey and St Albans and Hertfordshire Architectural and Archaeological Society.

9   N. Alvey, *Education by Election*, p. 2.

10   N. Alvey, *Education by Election*, title page.

11   The Asylum board could also allocate proxy votes to 'last-timers', children aged 10 who would no longer be eligible for admission beyond that age. Places could also be secured for a one-off payment of 100 guineas by a sponsor, the same regulations of eligibility being applied. Queen Victoria made a payment of 600 guineas to enable Edward, Prince of Wales, to secure a place for a child at each election for the rest of his life.

12   N. Alvey, *Education by Election*, p. 21.

13   London Orphan Asylum provision, quoted in N. Alvey, 'The London Orphan Asylum Clapton', *Terrier*, 1991, p. 2. Used with permission: N. Alvey.

14   N. Alvey, *Education by Election*, p. 21.

15   London Orphan Asylum provision, table quoted in P. Horton, *The London Orphan Asylum*.

16   Herbert Dixon (source), 'The Congo Mission', *The Freeman*, 2 September 1881. Used with permission: Baptist Union of Great Britain.

17   Reed's original vision of providing schooling as an end in itself had given way to the more commercially minded approach of the current governors by the time Herbert attended the orphanage school. Boys were trained for careers in commerce, the girls to be governesses and teachers. Help was given in finding jobs, and the orphanage supplied working clothes for leavers and gifts of £2 or £3 as a reward for good conduct in their first employment.

18   John 15:5, with punctuation as in KJV.

6

A Peculiar Place for Romance

'Life . . . is a journey; a journey that must be travelled, however bad the roads or the accommodation.'

Oliver Goldsmith, 1816[1]

Medical practice in mid-Victorian times appears primitive when compared with our modern technologies, plethora of qualifications and subdivisions of specialities. In 1878, when Elizabeth and Herbert stepped into University College Hospital, nurses and doctors were coping with very basic conditions. At the heart of the hospital was the operating amphitheatre, a facility fixed between hope and despair. On one side was the dispensary, on the other the postmortem examination room and the mortuary. Such was the mortality rate that wealthy patients were more likely to elect to have surgery on their kitchen table than in hospital. The room was as described – a theatre. Observers filled steeply rising horseshoe tiers of wooden benches to watch the surgeon and his assistants perform around the narrow table at its centre. It was also here that consultants came to teach their pupils their trade, my great-grandfather among them.

'Now gentlemen,' said the surgeon as he fumbled for his list of the students' names in the pocket of his old frock-coat, a smelly item that was turning green along the sleeves and was stiff with pus and blood. 'Foreign bodies in air passages. You, sir . . . supposing you were my house surgeon, which God forbid . . . ah, well, perhaps we will not suppose anything so painful. Suppose, then, you were in general practice and one fine morning three frantic females carrying an apparently dead child burst into your surgery and told you the child had been playing with a button, that the button had disappeared and the child was suffocating. Now what are you going to do?'

'Ah . . .'

'Hurry, man, the child is close to death.'

'I would chloroform the patient. Then proceed to sterilize the skin on the front of the neck . . .'

The consultant jumped up from the operating table, glared at him over the top of his gold rimmed glasses and pulled at his pointed beard, 'Confound it! If you're going to wait until you have done all that, sir, I should say you would save time by proceeding to the nearest undertaker and ordering a coffin.'

'The man with the leg in Ward 2,' he rounded on another student, 'your opinion?'

'An effusion into the bursa beneath the suprapatellar tendon, sir.'

'Housemaid's knee, eh? You, sir. Do you agree?'

The student had not the foggiest notion, 'Er . . . oh, yes, sir . . .'

'Well, how are you going to treat it?'

'Strap it, sir?' the student offered timidly while surveying the toes of his shoes.

'Tap it,' roared the consultant. 'Tap it! My dear fellow, if you are going to do things like this in your practice, you'll soon find yourself in police court.'

He pushed the list of names back into his pocket unread. 'We will proceed upstairs to Ward 4, where we have a mason, who has reportedly fallen from his scaffold twenty feet onto his head.'

And with that the consultant strode briskly out of the theatre with his retinue of students surging after him, while the dressers closed the sliding doors on another sorry session.[2]

Such were the humiliations of Herbert and his fellow students as they trailed from bed to bed and were asked to identify and treat the diversity of diseases and disorders that afflicted their patients. These sessions were, nonetheless, not without amusement. The hospital had attracted its fair share of eccentrics. Sherard Freeman Statham had been dismissed for his coarse manners and swearing, and for slapping a patient prepared for surgery on the buttocks. In Herbert's year of training, Christopher Heath, professor of clinical surgery, was another prime example of rudeness. The physician delighted in damning his inferiors 'like a gentleman'.[3] Despite this, or perhaps because of this, Heath had a good following, even if, from time to time, his students must wither under his trivializing tirades.

Herbert learned the basics of diagnostics: auscultation, inspection, palpation and percussion, or, in common parlance, listening, looking, feeling and thumping. He was introduced to the use of a stethoscope, the interpretation of thermometer readings, and the prescribing of medicines. At a time when pharmacists, keen to promote their businesses, were experimenting with all kinds of remedies, pharmacy was at best an imprecise science. Cure-alls such as Dr Thomas' Eclectric Oil [sic] and Holdroyd's Gravel Pills were popular. Oil of Earthworms, worms boiled in olive oil or wine, was prescribed for bruises. The Everlasting Pill, a small ball of antimony, was guaranteed to purge the gut with diarrhoea and vomiting. When swallowed and 'recovered' by one patient, the pill was cleaned and reserved for the next. Other concoctions were downright dangerous. Mrs Winslow's Soothing Syrup for infants was made with morphine, while Dr John Collis Browne's chlorodyne mixture for coughs and colds contained cannabis, chloroform and opium. Herbert was privileged, nevertheless, to be in a progressive London teaching hospital where teachers were eager to push forward the boundaries of medicine. Consultants and surgeons were continually on the lookout for 'interesting' cases, sometimes paying people a few pennies or a shilling to attend the hospital so that they could be examined.

Elizabeth also improved her competence on the wards. The motivation for all her actions was clearly set out in the Rules and Regulations of the sisterhood: 'Nurses must restrain themselves from all impatience with the sick under their care; treating all alike, whether thankful or unthankful, with gentleness and forbearance, remembering the words of Him who said: "Inasmuch as ye have done it unto one of the least of these, my brethren, ye have done it unto Me."'[4] 'Exact and prompt obedience'[5] to the instructions of medical staff and sisters was essential. She must be courteous at all times, rising from her seat if gentlemen of the committee, the chaplain or Sister Superior Gertrude Anna entered the ward, and she must be polite to all and sundry, including young student doctors.

My great-grandmother was required to trim the single gas lamp in each ward and manage the fire. Ward temperature was to be 60 degrees Fahrenheit and, when patients were sleeping, she must add 'small separate knobs of coal' to the grate, avoiding unnecessary noisy poking and raking. The windows were always kept open one inch at the top, for 'it is no substitute . . . to throw open the whole of the windows for an hour and set the whole ward sneezing and complaining of the cold'. She must keep the curtains around the beds tidily in position, protect the well-stuffed hair mattresses from rubbing on the iron bedsteads, and remove 'irritating particles'[6] from beneath the covers.

Elizabeth was instructed on how to deal with lice – 'more can be done by patience and soap and water than is generally allowed' – and lectured on the procedures for dressing patients, where 'male patients especially' should be encouraged to 'do such things as they can and ought to do themselves'.[7] She acquired a basic knowledge of anatomy, physiology, pathology and drugs. And she was expected to be able to act in an emergency if a physician was not present – although, perversely, some doctors were adamant that their nurses should not display too much initiative. In January 1880, *The British Medical Journal* set out a startlingly pompous opinion that the 'doctor is responsible for his patient; and the nurse must be a person who owes strict allegiance to him, who pays blind obedience to his orders, and pays it as absolutely as a private soldier the command of his superior officer'.[8]

Included in Elizabeth's nurses' manual was a set of recipes: brandy mixture, corn flour pudding with or without jam, calves foot jellies, a pottage of boiled fowl, stale bread and broth named chicken panada, and toast water (simply toast in water). There were also details of six ways of cooking an egg. She was provided with the instructions for concocting enemata, amongst them opium, tobacco and strong beef tea, directions for making fomentations of poppy and turpentine, and advice for preparing poultices of bread, charcoal and mustard. The bandages she applied were no less lethal than some of the medicines Herbert prescribed; double cyanide gauze was available in packs of 6 yards. Victorian water cures were popular. Elizabeth was taught to grade 'simple' baths into half a dozen categories from cold to hot. She prepared special baths such as the toxic mercurial vapour bath, where a patient, shrouded in a blanket that covered them to the neck, was required to sit on a cane-bottomed chair from under which fumes of heated calomel rose. Wrapping patients in wet sheets for up to an hour was also considered a good tonic. And then there were black, bloodsucking leeches to scoop from jars and apply to a patient's skin . . .

The hospital was a peculiar place to engage in a romance. The atmosphere hung with the stench of disease. Around the operating theatre, whiffs of chloroform, laughing gas and ether competed with the tang of new carbolic spray disinfectants. Unpleasant cleansing agents irritated the eyes, skin and throat. The hospital doors and drains allowed in rats, which gnawed and destroyed the dirty linen in the laundry. Daily, the 'great unwashed' trooped in and out of the waiting room; sick men, women and children propped up on wooden benches arranged like pews, or standing in queues for the dispensaries.

Etiquette demanded that the choreography of courtship must be danced, and Herbert and Elizabeth were no different to hundreds of Victorian young men and women who negotiated their steps to intimacy. The progress of their relationship, however, was hindered by the hospital's regulations. More often than not, they must have been limited to modest smiles by the side of an ill patient, glances across the table of the operating theatre or whispered conversations along the hospital corridors, where talking was not allowed. Herbert, nonetheless, with typical directness, made his feelings quickly known and secured the engagement of Assistant-Nurse Williams.

They made an attractive couple, linked not just by their love of medicine but by their personal spirituality and a sense of adventure. My great-grandfather was preparing to join a new initiative of the Baptist Missionary Society (BMS) on the Congo River. Elizabeth, having left St David's and her family behind, was eager to join him when the mission permitted them to be married. It proved to be a long engagement in which they had ample time to get to know each other. Elizabeth, I have no doubt, shared the stories of her family I have shared with you and Herbert, I am sure, told her tales about his forebears.

On Friday, 25 March 1785, a London-trained architect arrived in Broomfield, Essex, a farming community of about four hundred living in an assortment of timber-framed cottages spread along the main road from Chelmsford to Braintree. The man headed in the direction of the King's Arms, one of the community's two fifteenth-century inns. On the opposite side of the road stood an ungainly stud and plaster house with an undulating ridge of a roof. This was Well House, a Tudor property, which derived its name from the spring beneath its floors. It was Good Friday and Mr Robert Dixon, aged 27, was visiting his father and his grandfather, both widowers, who shared a home. Robert had come for a specific purpose. He was looking for a deeper spiritual experience and believed that the nonconformist churches would provide it. He wanted the blessing of his father, a staunch Anglican, to go and hear one of their preachers.

The two men exchanged pleasantries. Robert was not the first caller that day. Benjamin, his cousin, had also been to visit.

'He has strange notions in his head,' said his father. 'Running off to hear some dissenting preacher. A Mr Cooper, I believe. I hope you will not get such heresies into your head, Robert . . . or I will disinherit you!'

Robert hurriedly changed the subject. His father was clearly in no mood to listen to his request.

It was Tuesday morning before he plucked up sufficient courage again to return to Well House. He was determined to go to the nonconformist meeting. He must tell his father of his decision, whatever the consequences. His arrival was greeted with shocking news. Both his grandfather and his father had died in the night.

'The old gentleman went first. And in what circumstances! The doctor and nurse swear to it. They were sitting alongside his bed. Around midnight there was a knock at the bedroom door. Both heard it. The nurse, she went over and opened the door. No one was there. It happened a second time. And a third! The nurse looked up and down the landing. There was nobody. Nor nothing that would account for the knocking. Such was their dilemma that the good doctor was heard to swear.'

'It was the knocking for the death,' opined the doctor. 'Your grandfather passed away shortly after. And then, though I cannot credit it, not hours later I was called upon to view the corpse of your father. It is a strange affair, if ever there was one.'

These extraordinary events eliminated the obstacles to Robert's decision to abandon the Established Church for the nonconformists. As the sole beneficiary of his father's estate, he inherited over £10,000. And, with his choice of church, he also found a wife.

In an effort to make him feel welcome in nonconformist circles, local worshippers invited him to dine with them. Amongst the guests were William Lincolne and his sister, Rebecca. Rebecca was reluctant to go to the meal and said so. She was tired from the journey to her brother's home. More specifically, she was recovering from a troubled romance and had no wish to engage in frivolous conversation with young men, particularly not eligible ones.

'You are expected with me,' protested her brother. 'We are to meet Mr Dixon, a man of good property. He has recently joined us. We must make him welcome.'

Rebecca went but was singularly unimpressed with Robert, who kept them waiting for their supper and then arrived in his shooting outfit. She made her feelings clear to William.

'I have little liking for Mr Dixon, of good property or not. I find him a good deal selfish and not concerned for others at all.'

Robert, on the other hand, was very smitten with Miss Lincolne. Through her brother he arranged another meeting. Rebecca's second thoughts were obviously better than her first. Years later, in a letter to her son, she confessed, 'On the first of November [1785] Providence directed my path into the Company of your ever valued Father, an event marked with such mercy, care and goodness in my heavenly Father that I must ever acknowledge with gratitude.'

Within eighteen months, Robert and Rebecca, Herbert's great-grandparents, were married. They settled just north of Broomfield on the banks of the River Chelmer in a red-brick French chateau-style house with twenty acres of garden and pasture; a property that Robert designed and which was more than adequate to accommodate the couple's eight children. In one of the fields, Robert built a bath house with a thatched roof over a spring, and he kept a boat on the River Chelmer, where he fished for trout. He retired from architecture and, like his father, became a miller. Robert died in 1823, aged 66, and Rebecca was buried alongside him ten years later. In her final days she was surrounded by angels, strangely surprised that no one else in the room could see their divine shapes or hear their beautiful voices.

One of the most significant affirmations of Herbert's resolution to give himself 'entirely to God's service, and to go as a missionary to the heathen' came from a prayer written by one of his great-grandmothers. Perhaps this was Rebecca. In a letter written to one of his aunts, Herbert does not name this great-grandmother, simply describing her from a picture he had seen as 'half lost in her cap and frills'. Two days after he had made his decision to be a missionary, he had received a letter from this aunt. Herbert drew the letter out of the envelope, and with it a copy of the prayer on a slip of paper.

> It is our heart's desire and prayer that our children may be prais-
> ing God on earth when we are gone to praise him in heaven . . .
> Let not the light of our family religion be put out nor that treas-
> ure be buried in our graves, but let those who shall come after us
> do thee more and better service in their day, than we have done
> in ours, and be unto Thee for a name and a praise.

The 'coincidence' of the posting of this letter as he had prayed his prayer of commitment could not be ignored. He was, he felt, the answer to this 'grand prayer' written before he was born, and mused that it 'seems strange to me, that just when [my] prayer was answered I heard for the first time of [my great-grandmother's] prayer'. The timely arrival of his aunt's letter and his great-grandmother's prayer sealed his determination to be a missionary.

The paths that brought Elizabeth and Herbert together ran along familiar routes. Both families had their roots in fields, farms and milling. Both could trace back to ancestors such as George Williams and Robert Dixon, affluent men and leaders within their churches and communities, who exerted great influence on the direction of the Christian lives of their families. But their paths had also diverged. George Williams's fortune had risen out of tragedy, whereas Herbert's family had descended from prosperity into hardship. It is ironic that for many years Robert Dixon was the wealthy secretary of the Benevolent Society for the Relief of the Necessitous Widows and Children of Ministers in the County of Essex. He would have been distressed to learn that his great-grandson was reduced to life in an orphanage.

In 1880, my great-grandparents' paths parted company for a while. Herbert's training at University College Hospital came to an end and he left to work with the BMS, taking courses in carpentry and engineering to increase his usefulness on the mission field. His initial application to the BMS had not included any prospect of marriage. Elizabeth must wait until it pleased the committees of the mission to give their blessing. Her path would take her away from the hospital while Herbert, now ordained, embarked on the *SS Gaboon* to what Henry Morton Stanley, formerly John Rowlands, Elizabeth's childhood neighbour in Liverpool, described as 'Darkest Africa'.

NOTES

[1] Oliver Goldsmith, 'Letter XCIV', *The Miscellaneous Works of Oliver Goldsmith, M.B.: With Memoirs of his Life and Writings: Vol. 3 The Citizen of the World* (Glasgow: Chapman, 1816), p. 330. (Original quotation: 'The life of man is a journey; a journey

that must be travelled, however bad the roads or the accommodation'.)

2   Paraphrase of conversation based on a ward round conducted
by Christopher Heath, quoted in J.E. Francis, 'Fifty Years Ago.
A Round with Mr Christopher Heath', *UCH Magazine*, July
1949, 34, pp. 69–72. Used with permission: University College
London Hospitals NHS Foundation Trust.

3   Mobbs, a hospital porter, quoted in W.R Merrington, *University College Hospital and its Medical School: a History* (London:
Heinemann, 1976), p. 76.

4   Regulations of The Society of All Saints' Sisters of the Poor,
1862.

5   Regulations of The Society of All Saints' Sisters of the Poor,
1862.

6   Quotes in this paragraph from E.J. Domville, *A Manual for
Hospital Nurses*, pp. 8–10.

7   Quotes from E.J. Domville, *A Manual for Hospital Nurses*, p. 12.

8   'Nurses and Doctors', *The British Medical Journal*, 17 January
1880, p. 98. Used with permission: British Medical Journal.

7

Congo – Apart for a While

*'Going up that river was like travelling back to the earliest begin-
nings of the world, when vegetation rioted on the earth and the
big trees were kings. . . a great silence, an impenetrable forest.'*
                                                    Joseph Conrad, 1899[1]

There was, according to the Bakongo people, a land under
the sea. It was obvious to anyone with intelligence and a good
eye. To stand at the very edge of central Africa, where the
umber Congo River water meets the green of the sea, was to
know this was true. On 20 October 1881, the slim fingers of
the masts of the *SS Gaboon* touched the line of the horizon
and slowly grew in length until her tall funnel, belching black
smoke, appeared. A few minutes later the ship's prow broke
the waves and the ship steamed in towards land. It was a trick
which the white men performed frequently. The story of the
underwater land – a recent one, so Herbert learned – had
been embroidered with the threads of witchcraft. The victims
of sorcerers were to be found in the lands of the white men,
where they made cloth and served their new masters. Some
worked as labourers on the coast. Others, it was believed,
turned up as meat in the cans of food the white men brought

with them and consumed seemingly without qualm, much to the disgust of their African observers.

The *SS Gaboon* sailed on into the mouth of the Congo River, a seven-mile wide undivided estuary, stretching from the Portuguese Ponta do Padrão to the Dutch trading station at Banana. Padrão was the more attractive of the two peninsulas, 'a spit of marshy land covered with splendid forest and fringed with breakwaters of mangrove and clumps of beautiful Fan palms'.[2] Here Diogo Cão had raised a *padrão*, a stone pillar bearing the national coat of arms and a cross, to claim the territory for Portugal in 1482. Banana, on the other hand, was perhaps badly named. There was not a single banana plant the length of the narrow sandbar. It was just a mere 100 yards wide, populated by crows and occupied by factories. The latter were staffed by about forty Europeans and four hundred Africans – Kru from the Liberian coast, local Kabindas and Krumanos. The Krumanos were little more than slaves, enslaved as punishment for thieving from Europeans, or obtained from African chiefs willing to sell their own people for cloth, gin and guns.[3]

Herbert's travelling companion was an Irish missionary, Henry Crudgington, who was returning to Congo after a brief period in Britain. Already established in the Congo work were four other BMS missionaries – Thomas Comber and George Grenfell, the pioneers of the Congo mission, with William Holman Bentley and John Hartland, both from London. Comber, Grenfell, Bentley, Crudgington and Hartland represented the first wave of workers. Herbert, soon to be joined by another colleague, John Weeks, was seen as the first of a second company of arrivals, a fact which, in time, would ferment trouble between him and his new colleagues.

In the hold of the *SS Gaboon*, Crudgington and Herbert had stowed a two-masted steel whaleboat, the *Plymouth*. She had been built in six sections and could be reassembled with nuts and bolts. Crudgington and Herbert's first task was to navigate the whaleboat 100 miles upstream from Banana to the BMS's base station, Musuku. As far as I know, my great-grandfather had no knowledge of boats or navigating, and certainly not of the Congo. He must have been a very practical man, determined to give anything a try. Beyond Musuku, where the river was a cascade of cataracts, sixty Kru were to be employed to carry the four central sections, each weighing 300 pounds, on their heads to Isangila, the second riverside station, seventy miles away. The bow and stern, heavier at 500 pounds each, would be moved on 'trucks' – flat-topped trolleys hauled along the route. The *Plymouth* was an essential part of the BMS's ambitious plan to journey inland, establishing mission stations along the river as rapidly as possible. Sailing the safer waters between Isangila and the next station at Manyanga would avoid days of hazardous struggle through the jungle.

The voyage from the coast to Musuku proved a fascinating trip for Herbert. The riverbanks were marshy flats profusely decorated with clumps of red-purple orchids with light green spear leaves, which stood 6 feet tall, their colour reflected in the water. Dwarf palms provided hedges to small lagoons surrounded by mangroves roosting on thin legs, where red-beaked kingfishers and white egrets watched over agitated mudfish, and blue crabs burrowed into the black sand. On a trampled shore a crocodile watched them, a 'fixed smirk hanging about his grim muzzle'.[4] The interior, however, was hidden for the time being behind a seemingly impenetrable forest.

Herbert's role in this enterprise ceased at Musuku. From there he headed south-east, trekking for eight days along narrow avenues of elephant grass that reached up to 15 feet high, to the local capital, San Salvador (now Mbanza Kongo). In the trees above him perched an exotic menagerie of birds; red-headed barbets, black and white hornbills and blue rollers. There were medleys of parrots and woodpeckers that played hide-and-seek, nimbly moving to the unseen side of tree trunks whenever Herbert got close.

San Salvador stood on a broad grassy plateau nearly 2,000 feet above the river. It was an encampment of around two hundred huts made of sticks and grass standing beneath baobab trees with their ancient engorged trunks and emaciated branches, one of which carried the initials of Comber and Grenfell, carved on their first visit in 1878. To Herbert, arriving from London, the settlement of 1,800 inhabitants must have seemed of little significance. It had, however, occupied a position of prominence as the capital of the once thriving kingdom of Kongo and it was here that successful attempts to introduce Christianity to the region had been centred.

In the sixteenth century, San Salvador was a walled city, boasting a Roman Catholic cathedral and blessed with its own African bishop. Conflict with the Portuguese and then civil war robbed the city of its splendour, and it had been abandoned for a quarter of a century. Now reoccupied, the ruins of the city wall, shards of masonry 2 feet thick and up to 15 feet high, poked out of tangles of vegetation. The cathedral was roofless and bereft of its west front, the high altar covered in small ferns. As Herbert entered the city he noticed unnaturally straight lines of bushes marking the locations of villas lost to the undergrowth. The Kongo king, Dom Pedro V, who greeted his arrival, was reliant on levies from passing caravans and the gifts he received when bestowing the insignia of office on new rulers in the region.

Close to the city wall, an area the size of three football pitches had been cleared down to the red clay for the missionaries' compound. Hartland, the missionary in residence, showed Herbert to the house they were to share. It was a sizeable structure with dirt floors, built with rough stones taken from the old wall, and roofed with grass thatch. Adjacent were two or three huts which served as a school, and accommodation for the pupils. At the centre of the compound stood a palatial pigeon cote on six spindly, wooden legs. There was also a shed for the mission's donkeys and a paddock for ducks, hens, the goat, monkeys, pigs and sheep; 'a miniature dairy farm minus the butter and milk', as Herbert whimsically described it.

He had barely settled in to the house at San Salvador when letters from Britain informed him that Elizabeth was ill, probably suffering from typhoid. He was devastated. The news was 'very hard to bear . . . impossible to understand', he wrote. I can understand his turmoil. The letters from England must have taken six or more weeks to arrive. By the time Herbert received them he may, for all he knew, have already lost Elizabeth. He could only wait and pray for better news to arrive.

The hospitals of Victorian England were not safe places for their patients, nor for their staff. Over the two years of her training, Elizabeth witnessed the loss of 490 patients out of nearly four and a half thousand admissions. Young nurses, struck down with bronchitis, measles and mumps, sore throats and scarlet fever, left the profession through ill health in roughly equal numbers each year as they did for marriage. To make matters worse, the accommodation for the All Saints' nurses was in gloomy, cramped properties, condemned as 'totally unfit from a sanitary point of view'.[5] Typhoid struck the community in spring 1881 and Elizabeth's health gave way in the autumn. The remedy was to get out of London. She was sent to the home of a friend of Herbert's in Leamington, a town in central England famous for its water treatments. Relaxing in a world away from the jeopardies of London hospital life, she slowly began to recuperate in the town's Royal Pump Room Gardens.

Whether it crossed Herbert's mind as he prepared for the mission field that one day he would need to deal with the heartache of separation from his fiancée, I do not know. But this was the place God brought him to. Before he met Elizabeth he was already drawn to the Congo, an area receiving great attention through the exploits of Henry Morton Stanley. In 1877, the Welsh explorer completed a three-year expedition across the African continent, travelling from the east coast to the mouth of the Congo River. Over one hundred porters were lost through desertion, disease and drowning, or killed in stand-offs with hostile villagers. Stanley was the only one of the four white members in the company to survive. The terrain was harsh, the climate hostile, the welcome from village to village uncertain. Central Africa was no place for the faint-hearted.

While my great-grandfather fretted over Elizabeth, he was ill himself. On the route up to San Salvador he suffered a 'light' fever. On his arrival in San Salvador, the temperatures climbed to over 30 degrees and sapped his energy. He stumbled into lethargy and depression, and began to rely on quinine to lift him back to his language studies. He succumbed to a second fever, more severe than the first. This was followed by 'eczema' of both legs, rendering him lame for a month and unable to sleep.[6] When recovered, he was, nevertheless, characteristically cheerful, remarking, 'I have got off wonderfully well compared to many.'

Much to Herbert's relief, Elizabeth did not return to the hospital. From time to time she had been sent to nurse wealthier patients, who were willing to pay for her services in the sanctuary of their own homes. One of these had been the Duchess of Teck, Princess Mary Adelaide. 'Fat Mary' was a larger than life aristocrat in every way. Queen Victoria, who was her first cousin, despaired of her, noting that 'She is alas! [sic] grown enormous . . . she is so bright & happy . . . But her size is fearful!'[7] The Duchess's appetite for rich food was legendary. She complained bitterly when a doctor put her on a diet of Abernethy biscuits, a finer version of a seaman's hardtack, believed to be a remedy for digestive disorders. Elizabeth, perversely, was required to feed the Duchess 'strawberries and cream', words around which the Duchess rolled her 'r's with mouth-watering delight. Another patient had been a woman corn merchant and former mill owner, Maria Elphick, living in Reigate, Surrey. Mrs Elphick, although only 58, was in need of a full-time nurse. Elizabeth moved into the more lucrative sphere of private nursing and into the lady's distinctive property above her corn store close to the ruins of Reigate Castle. The move served Elizabeth well. Letters arrived in San Salvador informing my great-grand-father that she was 'looking wonderfully well . . . remarka-bly happy'. Herbert was exceedingly relieved, though he did remain frustrated with her for wanting to return to her first love of hospital work.

Herbert was soon absorbed in language study. Portuguese was the region's language of trade and formal communi-cation. Kikongo was the language of the locals; a sophisti-cated piling up of prefixes and suffixes in precise order which inflated simple words into ten or more syllables. Concise-ness was crucial; using a word incorrectly had been known to start a fight. My great-grandfather learned Kikongo from his daily encounters with the people of San Salvador, writing 'new' words into notebooks as he toured the area, dressed in a 'singlet, knickerbockers and stockings, boots and hat; occasionally a light jacket'.

'*E mundele, sumba nsusu?*'

Mundele was 'white man'. The man was holding a hen. *Sumba*? Or *nsusu*?

'*E mundele! Sumba mankondo?*'

This time the man had come with bananas. *Sumba* must mean buy. Hitched on the man's hip, hanging from a string that held up the rags around his waist, was a knife. He offered it to Herbert.

'*Sumba mbele?*'

Herbert hired three boys as servants. The boys, keen to learn English, were happy to exchange words to fill Herbert's notebook if he would tell them the English equivalents. Donkey was *ebuluku*. *Mpu*, the word for hat. *Diki* was one egg. *Meki*, more than one. *Kangilwa* was a frying pan. *Nsanga*, a necklace. *Sote*, a toad . . . There seemed to be a dozen words for cloth, depending on how it was worn, whether it had a fringe on one edge, was red or striped, or whether it was finely woven or rough for working in. This was a laborious method of language acquisition but one that the missionaries used rigorously. It was essential to prepare material for future workers and for work to begin on a translation of the New Testament.

In 1887, Herbert's colleague, Bentley published the fruit of the missionaries' note-taking, a dictionary of 10,000 words. Like every aspect of the work along the Congo, it would not have been possible without local Africans and African Christians. Mantantu Dundulu was a key figure in Bentley's translation work. The mission's first convert, aged just 12, he and Bentley collated each Kikongo word and its English equivalent, which made a pile of papers 10 feet high. Six years later, their New Testament was published by the British and Foreign Bible Society. This painstaking effort was clearly worthwhile. Kikongo was understood from the coast to the upper reaches of the Congo, encompassing a population of 2 million people.[8]

Each Sunday morning, Herbert rang a bell to call the residents of San Salvador to services held under the King's Council tree in the middle of the city. Numbers varied but often 100 adults turned out, King Dom Pedro occasionally gracing them with his presence. For ninety minutes the gathering sang in Kikongo to a harmonium and listened to one of the missionaries preach. Morning and afternoon Sunday schools were started and services held in a neighbouring town.

Every Sunday evening, my great-grandfather visited the king at one of his three homes to give him personal Bible instruction. The king was usually to be found sitting on a mat in his courtyard where people could come and consult him. He was a huge man in girth, relatively short in height. Normally he wore a cotton shirt and a loincloth that reached down to the ground. On occasions he adopted an incongruous fashion of Western dress, as startling as it was comical: a multicoloured jumper, a European-style jacket and a scarlet mantle, his head capped with a pith helmet. Around him were boys who acted as servants, listening in to Dom Pedro's conversations with Herbert. When the king received his meals of groundnuts, roasted plantains, pots of beans with a little meat or puddings made of cassava meal, he would eat and then let the boys divide the rest amongst themselves.

Herbert's medical expertise was put to good use; 'a most valuable weapon' in the effort to get established in San Salvador. In his first year he boasted that he had treated more than one thousand patients successfully. People would travel or be carried from as far away as six days' journey to see the white *nganga* (doctor). He also taught in the mission school but he was not a natural teacher, describing his school work in the summer heat as 'right down [sic] drudgery'. He had, however, high hopes that some of the thirty or so boys at the school would get baptized. Finding Christian and educated wives for his pupils presented a problem. Herbert, with colonial condescension, noted that only 'ordinary' Congo girls who knew 'how to make a farm and how to cook' were available. Women missionaries were needed to educate the girls. Herbert's solution was straightforward – his colleagues must return to Britain 'at the earliest possible opportunity' and get married; not an altogether altruistic proposal. According to Crudgington, my great-grandfather was in a 'fever heat'[9] to get home!

Herbert seems to have been most taxed by the fickleness of the king and the activities of Portuguese Roman Catholic priests. Dom Pedro juggled his favours, sometimes supporting the padres, at times the Protestants, and occasionally bestowing his approval in equal measure. Roman Catholicism was not truly Christian, as far as Herbert and his colleagues were concerned. Any embracing of the priests' teaching by Dom Pedro was greeted with despair and renewed calls to supporters in Britain for prayer. There were, Herbert believed, blatant attempts by the Portuguese to close down the BMS's efforts. A party of padres, wanting to re-establish work there, had arrived eight months before him, armed with a letter from the king of Portugal and an escort of marines. Herbert poured scorn on 'a most clumsy attempt to colonize the place' when four men, four women and five children arrived to start a farm. When the party mistreated African graves, people from a nearby town threatened to shoot them. It was all to the Protestants' advantage, noted Herbert somewhat superiorly, that the locals 'can see a vast difference between the English and the Portuguese'.

For the first few months, Herbert worked alongside Hartland before being joined by his newly arrived co-worker,

John Weeks. Hartland was anxious to get away. The primary focus was to push deeper into the centre of Africa. The mission stations at Musuku, Isangila and Manyanga were merely stepping stones along the river into the interior and the *Plymouth* not the only boat to be transported out from Britain. The objective was to establish a base at Stanley Pool (now Pool Malebo), a huge lake located at the top of the unnavigable rapids of the Congo River, beyond which the river course arced north and then drifted south for another 2,500 miles.

The strain that this rush for the interior of Africa placed on the small team of seven missionaries was colossal. Weeks and Herbert, the new missionaries, ministered at San Salvador, while Comber, Grenfell, Bentley, Crudgington and Hartland worked along the river. There was little respite. Supplies must be ferried up and downstream continually. Ill health sapped their energy. The team were heavily dependent on the cooperation of local Africans to achieve anything. While the London office scoured the chapels of Britain, encouraging young men to give up the comfort of their churches, the missionaries in the Congo were being stretched – physically, mentally and spiritually – to breaking point.

NOTES

[1] Joseph Conrad, 'Heart of Darkness', *Blackwood's Edinburgh Magazine*, London (1899).
[2] H.H. Johnston, *The River Congo from its Mouth to Bolobo with a General Description of the Natural History and Anthropology of its Western Basin* (London: Sampson Low, Marston, 1895), p. 15.

3 The export of Africans into slavery had ceased by the time Herbert arrived in the Congo, the practice being policed by British cruisers and curtailed by the loss of lucrative markets. There was, however, a thriving market for slaves within the Congo region, fuelled by the need of Europeans for cheap labour and the desire of local rulers to furnish themselves with material wealth.

4 H.H. Johnston, *The River Congo*, p. 27.

5 Report of University College Hospital Subcommittee, quoted in W.R. Merrington, p. 253.

6 This is Herbert's diagnosis of his condition.

7 Queen Victoria, quoted in J. Pope-Hennessy, *Queen Mary 1867–1953* (London: Allen and Unwin Limited, 1959), p. 31.

8 Mantantu Dundulu (ca. 1865–1938) went on to assist in a revision of the Bible in Kikongo (1926), assisted Mrs Hendrina Margo Bentley in a translation of the Proverbs and Psalms, helped translate a book on the life of St Paul and the Acts of the Apostles, translated a book entitled *Peep of Day* and wrote an autobiographical sketch. Posthumously he received the Royal Order of the Lion from the Belgian monarch.

9 Letter from H. Crudgington to the BMS, Baynesville Station, Congo, 3 October 1882.

8

Hell's Cauldron

'When Christ calls a man, he bids him come and die.'
Dietrich Bonhoeffer, 1963[1]

Hell's Cauldron, a huge confusion of seething water ten miles upstream from Musuku, where the Congo River turns abruptly south, was well named. It was mapped on Admiralty charts as having 'no bottom at 1,300 feet'.[2] Upstream the current raced out of a narrowing gorge and pitched its strength against a 200 foot sheer cliff face of red rock on the opposite shore. Impeded in its progress, the water boiled and seethed until it escaped south, scouring out a great bowl more than a mile in diameter. A visitor described the blurred reflections in the clear water as 'altogether suggestive of some awful Styx faintly tinged with the glow of hell fire'.[3] Overhead, against a backdrop of dark, purple-green forests on a jumble of hills, black vultures wheeled around in the unquiet air. At this scene of intense beauty and savage splendour, the BMS missionaries had built one of their mission stations.

Perched on a prominent knoll 200 feet above the Cauldron the missionaries had established a base, which, despite its position, they had paradoxically called 'Underhill'. It had been erected on the south bank of the river to replace the station at Musuku, and named after Dr Edward Bean Underhill, one of the worthy secretaries of the BMS. The site was in some respects a good one. The station was situated near a natural harbour and commanded a good view of what little river traffic there was in both directions. Nonetheless, it was isolated and fraught with peril. There was nothing as permanent as the stone house at San Salvador. The main building was a simple structure, stalks of dwarf palms nailed to a skeleton of stout poles cut from neighbouring trees. In the absence of a decent path it was hard to penetrate the tall grasses that hemmed in the compound on the cliff edge. The harbour was troubled by crocodiles and the station by snakes. Spitting cobras and black water snakes were a hazard. There were green snakes hiding in the undergrowth and slender brown snakes that imitated the branches of trees. During one stay, Crudgington discovered a python beneath his bed.

Eight months after his arrival in Africa, this was Herbert's home for two months in the summer of 1882. His complaints about the place seem to amount to no more than the lack of glazed windows and the irritations of the breeze that swept his letters from the table onto the damp clay floor while the ink was still drying. He had trekked upriver from San Salvador to help Crudgington and a team of Africans build the main house and storage huts. There was a considerable amount of merchandise to be ferried upstream. The local people requested payment for the land in bottles of gin and rum, but the missionaries refused. They would pay with trade goods: beads, cotton, knives and other useful items. For eight weeks Herbert and Crudgington supervised the bringing of 2,000 boatloads from the old station to the new before my great-grandfather returned to San Salvador. The circumstances and consequences of his second visit eight months later were far less agreeable. Herbert was to be one of the casualties of the crippling pressures that were to beset the Congo team.

My great-grandfather was one of the pioneers of the work of the BMS in the Congo. It was only three and a half years before his arrival that Comber and Grenfell first sailed up the 'river that swallows all rivers'.[4] The two men were missionaries in Cameroon but as news of Stanley's successful crossing of Africa emerged, they hurried south to Banana and from there secured passage to Musuku. Representations were made to Dom Pedro and again on a second visit in August 1878 with a party of seven West Africans, a Portuguese translator and a donkey named Jack, which Comber was keen to have numbered as 'staff'. The request to start a mission station at San Salvador was welcomed by the king. Comber sailed to Britain and recruited three new workers, Crudgington, Hartland and Bentley. This fervour over the Congo coincided with Herbert's studies at Regent's Park College, a Baptist training facility situated a short walk across the park from London's exotic zoological gardens. It is perhaps, therefore, no surprise that he felt drawn to the region and that the BMS were eager to approve his application for missionary service.

Reinforcement of Herbert's desire to serve in central Africa also came with a change of church while he was at University

College Hospital, a requirement possibly of his application
to the BMS. He moved from his gothic-style Congregational Church in Stamford Hill to Downs Baptist Chapel
at Clapton, a brown brick fortress a short distance from the
London Orphan Asylum, which dominated the badly lit
roads around it. Opened in 1869, the church had grown to
over five hundred members in ten years under the guidance of
its first pastor, Vincent Tymms. Tymms was keen to promote
missionary work and the church held regular meetings at
which missionaries spoke, collected money for the BMS, and
encouraged its members to go overseas. Significantly, Bentley
was a member of the church and already in the Congo.

Although the five other members of the missionary team
had been in the region only a couple of years longer than
Herbert, my great-grandfather was not considered one of 'we
originals' – Bentley, Comber, Crudgington and Hartland,
joined later by Grenfell. Herbert was the first of six recruits
that followed. The distinction looks petty in hindsight, but it
created a source of irritation between him and the rest of the
missionaries. As a consequence small incidents, complicated
by the problems of communicating with remote locations,
were allowed more importance than they warranted. Herbert's
desire to go back to Britain so soon after his arrival, ahead of
Crudgington and Hartland, was considered premature, even
allowing for his passion to marry Elizabeth. His restlessness
in San Salvador, apparent in his eagerness to help Crudgington set up Underhill, was attributed to his dissatisfaction
over his placement there and a feeling that San Salvador was
'too obscure for his talents'. Herbert did not always endear
himself to his fellow workers either. 'Dixon's reports have ever

been the brightest. You know how he has always given us to understand that we never got on so well, had such influence over the king and people etc. as he', Bentley complained to Crudgington.

It was, however, Herbert's troubles with the Portuguese that created real tensions. In March 1883, with the prospect of a Portuguese armed force arriving in San Salvador, he wrote a hurried note to Bentley at one of the river stations. He planned to come upriver to consult the other missionaries about the situation. Herbert was, Bentley said, 'thinking of leaving Congo'. Unfortunately, Herbert's message arrived alongside news that in London the Reverend Tymms was proposing that the BMS abandon the work in San Salvador. Bentley described this news as a 'thunderclap'. How was it that the London committee was discussing a matter that the senior Congo missionaries had not been consulted on? Why should the BMS missionaries 'run' before the Roman Catholics? Was it not contrary to 'the leading of God's hand'? The BMS had a good welcome from the people of San Salvador and the mission had shown its commitment to the city by placing Hartland, Herbert and Weeks there. Bentley and his colleagues concluded that my great-grandfather had been writing 'dissatisfied letters' home for his own purposes. Whatever the truth of the matter, after Herbert left San Salvador in April he never did return to the city, as Bentley had surmised.[5]

Readers of the annual report of *The Missionary Herald* in May 1883 would have rejoiced with the editors in the news of the 'difficult, but noble, enterprise' that was the BMS mission to Congo. The report noted that 'as the result of the sanctified toil of our brethren, our chain of stations is complete from the mouth of the Congo at Banana to the waters of the Upper River at Stanley Pool'. The second wave of six missionaries promised by London, of whom Herbert and Weeks were the first, was in Africa. All but one station, Underhill, was now staffed by two missionaries. Crudgington was in Britain to get married to a Miss Harriet Wales, who would engage in ministry amongst the Bakongo women. Grenfell was busy supervising the transport of *Peace*, a new steamer, upstream from Banana, ready to reassemble and launch her at Stanley Pool and take the gospel a further 1,500 miles into the centre of the continent. The news from San Salvador was good: 'The attendance at the day and Sunday schools is increasing – many of the boys are giving hopeful indications. The people hear gladly the message of the Gospel, and the surrounding tribes welcome the missionaries.' It made good reading over an English breakfast.[6]

The sentiment of the annual report was praiseworthy but misplaced. Before the article was published, one of the newest recruits, William Doke, was dead and the mission on the Congo River was plunging into crisis. Doke's death was a double blow. Not only was he a loss to the day to day maintenance of the mission's initiative to push on upriver, but he had been specifically recruited as an engineer to aid Grenfell with the *Peace*. He and Grenfell had been involved with the boat's construction at Chiswick and her testing on the River Thames. Arriving in Banana in the New Year, he survived just three and a half weeks before succumbing to a fever.

Hartland was the second to die. With four years' service and due to return to Britain for a break, he was considered a veteran of the Congo mission and another sore loss to his colleagues. In April, falling foul of dysentery at Manyanga, he had travelled downstream to get help. The move proved superfluous. By the middle of May he was dead. Henry Butcher, another of the new recruits, described it as 'a serious breach . . . in our ranks'.[7]

Butcher was himself the third fatality of the year. In October, while working alone, he fell into delirium and, unable to prescribe treatment for himself, quickly passed away. The threads of the mission that had been so ambitiously sewn into the string of stations were breaking one by one. Grenfell wrote home, lamenting the situation, 'Here we are scarcely knowing which way to turn, and I only wish I could see a speedy way out of our difficulties. If more men don't soon come, the Congo Mission will collapse, and the work that has cost so much will be thrown away.'[8] The deaths of these three men were not the only losses to the work. By the time Butcher died, the mission had already lost a fourth worker – my great-grandfather.

While Weeks laboured away in San Salvador, continuing to build the mission premises, teaching and preaching, running a basic printing press, acting as doctor and fulfilling every other role required of him, Herbert left the city in April, as he had informed Bentley he would. He took the path down from the plain and found a boat to take him as far as Underhill, where

Grenfell was currently working while Crudgington was in Britain. As Herbert climbed up from the quayside it was clear that his colleague was in poor health. Grenfell had been at the station for nearly three months and the conditions had taken their toll. For four weeks he had been suffering with dysentery and was in desperate need of a change of location. Herbert put his plans to go further upriver on hold. He would remain at Underhill until Crudgington returned. Grenfell was bundled into a hammock and transported upstream for recuperation.

As time passed, the unintended delay in his plans began to unbalance Herbert's usual optimism. While his new servant, Myala, and the other Africans with him slept, he wrote into the night, disturbed as the 'rude roaring of the mighty Congo rushing past the Mouth of Hell, mingles with the never ending "booming" of the Great Yalala Falls'. Between April and August he was sick six times and became anxious to return to the better conditions of San Salvador. The work was crippling. The link of stations must not be broken if supplies were to keep moving upriver to support those higher up and further in. As each boat brought loads to the harbour, Herbert forced himself to get up from his sickbed and supervise the unloading under the heat of the sun. Violent pains racked his back and he began to vomit violently. Myala made hot tea to help his fevers but nothing alleviated his condition. The illness put an acute strain on his heart, which began to fail, causing his legs to swell with severe oedema. He became weaker and weaker. His feet were paralyzed. By September he was no longer able to stand.

When Crudgington and his wife arrived unexpectedly at Underhill in early September they found Herbert, as he later joked, literally on his last legs. Crudgington was blunt in his assessment. Herbert must return to Britain as soon as he could be carried down to Banana, or he would die. Less than two years after the *SS Gaboon* had broken the horizon and sailed into the mouth of the Congo, the Dutch steamer *Africaan* dropped beneath the waves, leaving Africa behind. In a letter to the BMS, Herbert described the voyage, 'The weariness and pain of those days seem now like some hideous nightmare. The only gleam of light being the loving kindness of God, who kept me from once doubting His love and faithfulness – earth seemed to be past, and I was going home indeed.'[9]

NOTES

[1] D. Bonhoeffer, *The Cost of Discipleship* (New York: Macmillan, 1963), p. 99. Used with permission: SCM Press.

[2] Quoted in W.H. Bentley, *Pioneering on the Congo: Volume 1* (New York: Fleming H. Revell, 1900), p. 450.

[3] H.H. Johnston, *George Grenfell and the Congo: Volume 1* (London: Hutchinson, 1908), p. 271.

[4] The 'river that swallows all rivers' is taken from the Kikongo name for the river *Nzadi* or *Nzere*, from which the Portuguese derived the name Zaire, subsequently used for the name of the Democratic Republic of the Congo between 1971 and 1997.

[5] Quoted material above taken from letter from W.H. Bentley to H. Crudgington, Congo, 20 March 1883.

[6] Quoted material above taken from 'The Congo – Central Africa', *The Missionary Herald*, 1 May 1883, pp. 168–171.

[7] Letter from H.W. Butcher to Revd J. Penny, Congo, undated, quoted in 'The Congo Mission', *The Missionary Herald*, 1 October 1883, p. 349.

8 G. Grenfell, Manyanga, Congo, 30 October 1883, quoted in G. Hawker, *The Life of George Grenfell* (New York: Fleming H. Revell, 1909), p. 155.

9 Letter from H. Dixon to A.H. Baynes, Canonbury, London, 19 November 1883, quoted in 'The Congo Mission', *The Missionary Herald*, 1 December 1883, p. 404.

9

A Most Suitable Match

'Press forward. Do not stop, do not linger in your journey, but strive for the mark set before you.'

George Whitefield, c. 1739[1]

My great-grandfather was found lodgings in a respectable villa on the banks of the New River in the suburbs of north-east London, close to the quaint, circular, brick watch hut that still overlooks the waterway. He was in a bad way. It was feared that he might never walk again. His feet and legs were useless. He was given the support of doctors provided by the BMS, and had the help of friends; the house was less than two miles from his church, Downs Baptist Chapel. He also had the attentions of a private nurse to care for him. Elizabeth left her post in Reigate and moved to London. After their two years apart, my great-grandparents were able to renew their courtship and Elizabeth was there to help Herbert with the devastating disappointment that was on his horizon.

New River was, in fact, neither new nor a river. It was an early seventeenth-century canal curving between tree-lined banks, bringing fresh water from chalk springs in Hertfordshire into the heart of London. This narrow, tranquil watercourse provided a sanctuary beside which to recuperate, just as Elizabeth had found a place to convalesce at Leamington. Herbert began to find strength in his legs and feeling in his feet. After six months he was able to stand and move around a little with the aid of crutches. He was, however, not a patient man. He was determined to marry as soon as possible and return to the Congo. In the minutes of a Downs Chapel meeting in February 1884 I found Herbert's robust reply to a congregation of over three hundred when he was questioned about his future:

> Some people had said 'Of course you won't go back to the Congo'. To these, said [Herbert], I have replied, 'I would rather die than not go back to my work there . . . I found a joy in work there I never had before, and did not know could be enjoyed in this world' . . . it will be a happy day to me when the Committee of the Baptist Missionary Society says 'Go, take up your work again with the brethren on the Congo.'[2]

His doctors strongly disagreed. They would not sanction Herbert going to Africa again. The missionary force in the Congo had continued to lose workers through sickness and death. Although he continued to improve, my great-grandfather represented too much of a risk to his own health and a burden on the resources of the frail Congo mission.

It had always been Herbert's intention to return home to marry Elizabeth, anticipating that the two of them would sail for Congo once the BMS accepted my great-grandmother as a candidate. The BMS's acceptance of the doctors' opinions threw both Herbert's future and his marriage plans into disarray. It was not possible to marry without permission and yet, if Herbert did not have a designated place on the mission field, how could he apply for permission? The BMS would not agree to accept Elizabeth if they did not know for which country they were testing her suitability. The only apparent alternative was for Herbert to resign from the society. So much was at stake. His intended life's work, his obedience to God, and his desire to marry after four years' engagement were being frustrated by circumstances he could not resolve.

Herbert's disappointment at the committee's decision is evident. A meeting with them reiterated what he already knew. There was little point, even foolishness, in requesting permission to return to the Congo. He found 'this fresh providence of God' harder to bear than his illness. He decided, nonetheless, to say no more on the matter. God, he accepted, had shut the door to Africa for him and Herbert would not try to open it again. God, however, once again stepped into the story.

Two days after Herbert had been informed of the doctors' decision, he received a letter. It had been posted some weeks earlier from a city in the north of China. The writer was another BMS missionary, Arthur Sowerby, who was working with his wife, Louisa, in the provincial capital of Shanxi Province, Taiyuan. Sowerby and Herbert had a lot in common. They came from the same area of London and had studied together at Regent's Park College. When Sowerby read of Herbert's illness he had been 'moved by some impulse, whose strength apparently surprised him'. Sowerby considered that the climate in Taiyuan would be significantly healthier than the Congo, and 'the land with all its vast moral sores and spiritual destitution was crying for Christians to go over and help them'.

Sowerby's proposal echoed an option that the doctors had already recommended, a move to Japan or north China. Herbert seized the initiative and wrote to the BMS. If he could not go to the Congo, then he wanted to go to China. More specifically, he wanted to go to the city of Taiyuan to join Sowerby. And he asked the committee to consent 'to my going out married'. He had, he considered, completed his probation in the Congo and Elizabeth, with her nursing skills, would 'prove a real helper' in the work they wanted to do.[3]

Two weeks later, he received a reply from the secretary of the BMS, Alfred Baynes:

My dear Mr Dixon,

It is now my official duty to inform you, in reply to your letter dated 'Cambridge, 7th July', that, in pursuance of the very hearty recommendation of the China & Japan & Western Sub Committees, the General Committee of the Society on Wed[y] last sanctioned your request to be permitted to labour in China as a Missionary of the Society, as your return to Africa has been so clearly barred by medical testimony. You will be glad, I am sure, to know that the decision of the Committee was unanimous. They felt that in the presence of the medical certificates of D[rs] Roberts and Gowers, it would be most unwise to sanction your return to the Congo; and as China is mentioned by the Doctors as presenting probably the most suitable field for the future for you to work in, the Committee have decided that you should be appointed to work in that Empire, and be stationed in Taiyuan.

Baynes's letter contained more good news. '[The committee] therefore consent to your marriage with Miss Williams.'[4] In

St David's it was time for the *gwahoddwr* to sling his bag on his back once more and begin his round of gathering wedding gifts.

It is easy to imagine the news spreading around the Treginnis Peninsula that Thomas Williams's daughter was coming home to wed her missionary husband. I can feel her parents' pride and delight at seeing her back in St David's after her years away from Wales. Elizabeth, however, chose to marry in her 'beloved' Llys-y-frân, a small village strung like a tiny bead on the web of pathways north of Haverfordwest, a day's walk from her family home. This was the village of her maternal grandmother and the place where her uncle George had settled as minister after leaving the Tabernacle Chapel in St David's.

On 1 November 1884, Elizabeth arrived in the village. Half a mile along the road, adjacent to a sturdy, stone-built 'British Schoolroom', stood Gwastad Chapel, a cavern of a building crammed with pews but well served with six large 'church' windows to let in what there was of the autumn sun. Ahead of her on the road was a group of children, anticipating her arrival.

'You may not pass until you have paid,' chorused the children.

The custom of *Dala Cwentin*[5] obliged both her and Herbert to pay before being allowed to proceed. Elizabeth, as required, threw down a handful of coins and watched the children scatter like mice to collect their reward. Then she walked on with her father to her wedding.

I have walked along the small lanes that my great-grandparents walked that day. Gwastad Chapel is still there. As I entered the porch, with its grey door and diagonal rows of white painted coat pegs, I could visualize the wedding day. The two narrow aisles that run either side of the chapel left little room for the bride and her father to walk in together. Waiting in the cramped space at the front of the church was Uncle George, clothed in his black minister's suit, his fine head of hair and beard now turning white, his deep-set eyes as dark as ever. It was a special moment. Of the few letters of my great-grandmother that remain, one is to her uncle George expressing her love for him and the village. I imagine Herbert standing alongside him, turning to greet Elizabeth. A short while later they were together at last, emerging from the solemnness of their vows onto the lanes of Llys-y-frân, and I traced their footsteps down the road to China.

NOTES

[1] George Whitefield (1714–1770), 'The Folly and Danger of Being Not Righteous Enough', a sermon preached at Kennington-Common, Moorfields, and Blackheath, London, http://www.ccel.org/ccel/whitefield/sermons.xi.html (accessed 18 November 2013).

[2] 'Church Meeting Minute Book 1883–1898', Downs Baptist Chapel, 14 February 1884, p. 14. Used with permission: Open Doors Baptist Church.

[3] Quoted material above taken from letter from H. Dixon to A.H. Baynes, Cambridge, 7 July 1884, quoted in minutes of the BMS Western Committee, 15 July 1884, pp. 209,210,211.

[4] 'Letter from A.H. Baynes to H. Dixon, London, 21 July 1884.

[5] Literally 'to catch Quentin'. The name 'Quentin' may have origi-
nated with the upper classes, as only wealthier families would
have been able to give money in this manner.

10

Shanxi – Travelling West of the Hills

'Our lines here have fallen in rather pleasant places.'
Herbert Dixon, 1887[1]

Amongst the very few photographs I have of my great-grand-parents is a small, sepia card. On the reverse is the photographer's address in English and Chinese, set against a background of exotic flowers. On the front is a fine portrait of Herbert, resplendent in Chinese dress.

Elizabeth and her new husband, like their missionary colleagues, discarded the clutter of Victorian fashion in an attempt to integrate into Chinese society. Herbert removed his shirts and put on sleeveless jackets with high manda-rin collars. Beneath these he wore tailored silk gowns which stretched to his ankles and had sleeves that hung a foot beyond his fingertips. He changed his breeches for pairs of cotton leggings tied at the ankle, each leg independent of the other, and hid the shyness of his receding hairline with a tight fitting, black silk cap topped with a red knotted Chinese button. He also shaved off his beard, retaining a neat, but very droopy, moustache; a concession to the fad adopted by many of the Chinese men he would have to deal with. Elizabeth's costume was no less distinct. Fussy dresses with bustles were shed for loose open-sleeved jackets. She wore silk for formal occasions, blue calico for everyday wear. These she combined with modest ankle-length skirts, beneath which her heavy leather footwear was exchanged for quaint satin shoes with thick paper soles. Together they made a well turned out, if somewhat unusual, Chinese couple.

My great-grandparents were in honeymoon mode, happy to be together in 'rather pleasant places'. The excitement of their wedding, the encouragement of their valedictory service, and the exhilaration of setting out for Asia meant that little was able to cloud their horizons. They sailed from Southampton on 28 January 1885 on a newly built Glen Line steamer, the *Glengarry*. The ship was taking advantage of the lucrative China tea trade, the recently opened Suez Canal, and a considerable number of Chinese coolies, who collectively were willing to pay £1,000 to sleep like prover- bial sardines on deck or in the ship's hold. En route to Shang- hai, the ship docked at Singapore, allowing Herbert and Elizabeth the opportunity to explore this 'Liverpool of the East' for two days. They were shuttled around the island in *jinrickshas*, bamboo carts with two large wheels reliant on coolie pulling power. Sometimes they took more intrepid rides in *gharries*, horse-drawn cabs. In these the driver, seated precariously on the wooden vehicle shafts, dismounted and remounted whenever the horse required instruction to turn a corner; all without reducing speed. They were fascinated by barbers shaving the crowns of pigtailed customers, amused by Chinese men in traditional gowns wearing European hats, and bemused by painters whitewashing houses without the aid of a ladder. They wondered at girls bathing in 'Nature's garments', and were amazed at the cheapness of strange fruit – pineapples, bananas, coconuts and 'stringy and sickly' sugar cane.[2] Around 10 p.m. on the first evening, Herbert chanced upon one of the island's tailors and impetuously ordered two white suits.

'They must be ready for 12 noon tomorrow,' Herbert was adamant.

There would be no problem, the tailor assured him in pidgin English. The suits were duly delivered on time but needed alterations.

'We leave at eight in the morning,' Herbert insisted.

'No problem,' the man reiterated and hurried away.

It was midnight when Herbert and Elizabeth were awoken by knocking on their cabin door. My great-grandfather tumbled out of his berth and opened the door to the tailor. The suits were finished. Would the Teacher like to try them on? And, if the Teacher was satisfied . . . payment could be made.

Elizabeth was not a good sailor in the worst of weathers. In the South China Sea, the *Glengarry* slued and yawed around its compass for a week, heaving and groaning through the pummelling of an unrelenting storm. She lay in her berth, delirious for several days. It was some relief, no doubt, when she was able to disembark at Shanghai, two months after their departure from England. The journey, however, was far from over. She and Herbert transferred to a smaller vessel that coasted another 600 miles further north, where the weather settled to the bluster of hot, dry winds and the pleasure of warm days and cool nights. Finally, their ship rounded the Shandong Peninsula and eased between a procession of outlying islands and a range of low lying hills into the natural harbour at Chefoo (now called Yantai).

Chefoo, a city on the northern shores of Shandong Province, had provided an important stepping stone for the BMS's missionary activity in China. Protestant mission had, regrettably, arrived in the wake of the gunboats of the British navy following the first 'Opium War' in 1842, a war which future prime minister Gladstone described as 'unjust in its origin, a war more calculated in its progress to cover [Britain] with permanent disgrace'.[3] The treaty that followed forced open five of China's ports to Western trade and ceded Hong Kong to Britain. A second 'Opium War' in 1856 left China vulnerable to more demands for more concessions. New ports, including Chefoo, were unlocked to foreign trade under the Treaty of Tianjin. Significantly, the settlement also allowed foreigners to travel throughout China, whereas previously they had been confined to the treaty ports. Missionaries, not content to reside in designated coastal areas, began to push their way into the country's interior, avidly recording the lives and locations of potential converts in words and photographs that were sent back to Britain for publicity and prayer.

The BMS was one of the missionary societies to take advantage of the Tianjin settlement, resolving that this 'providential' openness of China 'constitutes an urgent call upon the churches of Christ to send missionaries to that great country'.[4] In 1859, two couples, members of other missions, transferred to the BMS and worked in Shanghai with limited success.

Two years later they moved their base to Chefoo. Threats from bandits and ill health plagued the missionaries' efforts. Of the five couples appointed by the mission, two of the men and one woman died while their spouses and the other two couples, unable to cope with the demands of missionary life, left the work. Even though a Baptist chapel with a membership of thirty-five was established in the town, by 1870 the BMS mission in China had been reduced to one unmarried representative, Reverend Timothy Richard; a man who had a significant, though not necessarily always positive, impact on the lives of my great-grandparents.

Richard, born in south Wales a decade before Elizabeth, was an extraordinary individual. One of his biographers noted that had 'he died in China his funeral would have been the greatest of any foreigner'.[5] Another historian described him as 'one of the greatest missionaries whom any branch of the Church . . . has ever sent to China'.[6] Richard was under no illusions as to the problems he faced if the BMS work was to progress. Shortly after his arrival, a group of Roman Catholic nuns were raped and killed in Tianjin by a mob, who believed the women were mistreating Chinese orphans in their care. A month later a meeting at Chefoo's nonconformist Union Church was not held on 'account of the commotion and excitement caused by the rumours that the Chinese were about to massacre all the foreigners in Chefoo'.[7] Richard, however, had no intention of going home. He pursued his work in Shandong Province with restless energy. Chefoo seemed too well served by other missions to warrant the ministry of another society, so he moved to the inland city of Qingzhou, 180 miles south-west, which was a Shandong religious centre for Buddhists, Taoists and Muslims. Richard attracted a welcome from his new neighbours for his medical skills and death threats for his audacity in proclaiming his 'foreign' religion.

The first converts, a silk weaver and his wife, were baptized before the year was out and the church began to grow rapidly. Within three years, Richard, aided by another BMS missionary and a Chinese pastor from Chefoo, registered 1,000 Chinese for baptism, and baptized 300 believers.

In 1877, Richard's reputation for care for famine victims brought him an invitation from the International Famine Relief Committee in Shanghai to travel further inland to Shanxi, a province the size of England and Wales and home to 14 million Chinese. The harvests across north China had failed. People, their faces grey with hunger, were reduced to stripping the bark from trees and mixing powdered stone with millet husks for food. Cartloads of women and girls were being driven into prostitution in exchange for bread. Wherever Richard went there were unburied bodies and tales of cannibalism. Across the region's provinces the disaster claimed a reported 15 million lives. Richard and his colleagues, Protestant and Roman Catholic missionaries working with Chinese officials, were credited with saving 70,000 of Shanxi's population from starvation. In 1878, the first Protestant church was opened in Taiyuan, the provincial capital. It was adorned with a large plaque inscribed in gold, 'The Hall of Universal Salvation', a gift of the local population in gratitude for the missionaries' work. It was here at Taiyuan that Herbert's college friend, Arthur Sowerby, had joined Richard and here that Herbert and Elizabeth began their lifelong commitment to work alongside the people of Shanxi.

The journey from Chefoo to Taiyuan took the best part of a month; over five hundred miles of well-worn, dust-encrusted country roads, moving from one primitive inn to another on foot, horseback or transported in small boats along rivers. Elizabeth was loaded into what Herbert described as 'a box slung between a front and hind mule, something in the manner that bobbies at home arrange for the comfort of incapable drunkards'. His jibe at Elizabeth's expense was somewhat tempered by his own misfortunes – a tumble from his horse down a 20 foot bank; an unpromising start to his horse-riding career.

I cannot imagine how Elizabeth dealt with the crudity of their accommodation each night. She must have had a great spirit of adventure and perseverance to share Herbert's sense of humour over their journey – 'a pleasant one as far as might be in this part of China'. Their rooms contained nothing but a wooden table, a few chairs and 'any amount of dirt'.[8]

Every evening she would have to lie down among the smells and snores of a dozen or more unwashed sleepers, who squeezed together as closely as possible on the 'beds'. These were rough brick shelves, called *kangs*, which were built with a stove beneath them. In winter the fumes from the coal fire threatened to suffocate the occupants, and in summer rats kept them awake. Travelling in spring, Elizabeth and Herbert could well have suffered both misfortunes.

My great-grandparents crossed Shandong and then Hebei Province to the mountains which border Shanxi. (Shanxi means 'west of the hills'.) From there it was still another 100 miles through the valleys of the Taihang Mountains, a range of peaks rising to 9,000 feet. Beyond the mountains they reached a fertile river plain, where in good years Chinese farmers harvested beans, barley, millet, oats and wheat twice a year, and cultivated orchards of apricots, dates, grapes, peaches, pears and persimmons. They found themselves on time-worn tracks that trekked unhurriedly along yawning valleys; stunningly long gorges with sheer sides, some as deep as 50 or 100 feet. These had been cut by centuries of wind and rain into the yellow-brown loess sand, a porous soil that crumbled easily between their fingers.

They travelled on through villages composed of brick houses and larger properties with castellated walls, some with towers standing as tall as 50 feet, strangely reminiscent of the country churches they had left behind in Britain. Nonetheless, St David's, the Congo and their life in the suburbs of London were already becoming a distant memory as the reality of their new work was revealed. The spiritual battle they faced was evident. Shrines populated the roadsides. In every town and hamlet there was a pagoda to protect its inhabitants against evil spirits. Around ancient acacia trees they saw altars of incense pots and candlesticks, the branches laden with flags, and red banners daubed with prayers in thick black ink. Finally, they came to the daunting walls of Taiyuan, 50 feet high, 40 feet thick and 8 miles in perimeter. It was a city of broad unmade roads, and closely packed houses and shops with concave tiled roofs, most of them in a general state of disrepair. Dominating the centre of the city was the governor's *yamen*, a lofty complex of official offices and homes fronted by a huge wall bearing the picture of a colossal and furious dragon.

Wearied by their journey, Herbert and Elizabeth were taken to Sowerby's family home. Sowerby and Louisa, his wife, were, temporarily, the only senior BMS missionaries in Taiyuan. Timothy Richard, now married, was on furlough in Britain with his wife, Mary. Two other senior missionaries, Joshua and Anna Turner, were settled in the city of Xinzhou, a day's journey north on horseback, two days away by cart. The last member of the team and the third new recruit was Evan Morgan, from Wales, who was glad, no doubt, to find another Welsh-speaker in Elizabeth. It was left to the Sowerbys to introduce my great-grandparents to life in Taiyuan, find them accommodation, provide teachers for language study, and for Arthur Sowerby to take Herbert out on his pony to visit the four stations he and his colleagues had established in the surrounding villages.

Before leaving London, or perhaps in one of the cities along the route, Herbert acquired the luxury of a newfangled technology, a typewriter. Despite some of his contemporaries considering the device far too cold and formal for a personal letter, he was happy typing letters home. It was six weeks, he reported, before they were able to move into their new home, a large property owned by a hermit of a landlady, which had stood empty for fifteen years and which they must share with Morgan. The house was on a main thoroughfare, where the wooden gates kept 'noisome smells and disgusting sights and uncouth tones'[9] at bay. They could boast of having two courtyards. The sanctuary of the inner one was for their own use and the other for servants, ponies, and a cow and calf. It was impossible, they were informed, to milk a cow unless there was a calf in attendance. The rooms had brick floors and whitewashed walls and they were 'blessed with verandahs'. The windows were divided into small squares of thin paper, which 'when it rains and blows', Herbert seems enthralled to have discovered, 'melts away delightfully'. He does not record his wife's opinion!

Herbert was also as enthusiastic and optimistic as ever about the prospects for mission. 'Results,' he wrote to the BMS six months after their arrival, 'we will talk about when harvest times comes; at present it is seed time, and we are concerned that the sowing be done largely and well.' Elizabeth busied herself with buying new clothes and the hiring and instruction of servants, while Herbert found ponies at around three pounds apiece and organized workmen to repaint the inner courtyard, construct additional doorways and build new chimneys. Two trees were ordered from a local gardener to begin the transformation of the place from 'wilderness' to 'quite bright and homelike'.[10]

They were also happy for another reason. Elizabeth's change into loose-fitting jackets had proved timely. Conceived somewhere on the voyage from Southampton to Shanghai, Elizabeth was pregnant with their first son, my grandfather, Thomas Benjamin Dixon; thereafter, inexplicably, 'Benjie' to his mother and 'Bennie' to his father.

NOTES

[1] Allusion to Psalm 16:6.

[2] Quotes this paragraph from 'A Portsmouth Missionary in China', *Hampshire Telegraph and Sussex Chronicle*, 9 May 1885.

[3] *Hansard*, Third Series, Volume 53, 1840, p. 818, http://hansard. millbanksystems.com/commons/1840/apr/08/war-with-china-adjourned-debate#column_818): contains Parliamentary information licensed under the Open Parliament Licence

Old Cross, St David's by Thomas Tudor, 1835.
Used with permission: The National Library of Wales

BMS compound, San Salvador, Congo, c. 1880.
The Missionary Herald, October 1880; used with permission: BMS

**Evangelist Chao,
c. 1901.**
The Missionary Herald, April
1901; used with permission:
BMS

**Herbert and
Elizabeth Dixon
family,
c. 1889.**
The Missionary Herald, December 1890; used with permission:
BMS

**Postcard from Elizabeth Dixon to Benjie, Shanghai,
14 June 1899.** Source: P. Bell

Xinzhou missionaries, c. 1900.
Back row, l to r: Dixons, Renaut, McCurrachs.
Front row: Sowerby, Ennals.
The Missionary Herald, August 1900; used with permission: BMS

Xinzhou East Gate, site of martyrdom.
The Missionary Herald, November 1908; used with permission: BMS

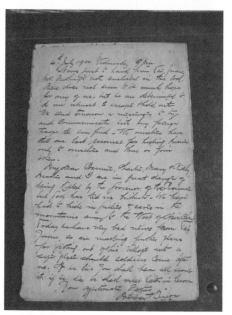

Herbert Dixon's last
letter to his children.
Source: P. Bell

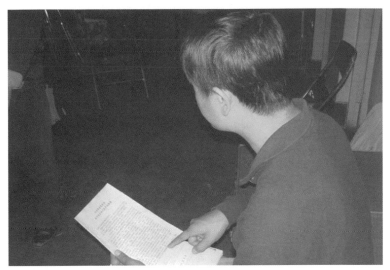

'It's a miracle!' Zhang, Xinzhou, 17 October 2006.
Souce: P. Bell

Xinzhou memorial site.
Source: Xinzhou church

Chinese inscription, Xinzhou memorial site.
Source: Xinzhou church

Old missionary house built by BMS missionaries, c. 1900, Xinzhou. Source: P. Bell

Old Xinzhou church built by BMS missionaries, c. 1900.
Source: P. Bell

**Modern
reconstruction
of Chinese
city gate.**
Source: Xinzhou church

Xinzhou church, 2006.
Source: P. Bell

Pru and Stuart with local Christians in new Xinzhou church, 17 October 2006. Source: P. Bell

v1.0 – http://www.parliament.uk/site-information/copyright/open-parliament-licence/ (accessed 13 December 2013).

4   BMS General Committee resolution, 20 April 1859, quoted in H.R. Williamson, *British Baptists in China 1845–1952* (London: The Carey Kingsgate Press, 1957), p. 20.

5   W.E. Soothill, *Timothy Richard of China: Seer, Statesman, Missionary and the Most Disinterested Adviser the Chinese Ever Had* (London: Seeley, Service, 1924), p. 19.

6   Dr K.S. Latourette, quoted in H.R. Williamson, *British Baptists in China 1845–1952*, p. 253.

7   Minutes of Union Church, Chefoo, quoted in H.R. Williamson, *British Baptists in China 1845–1952*, p. 32.

8   E.H. Edwards, *Fire and Sword in Shansi: The Story of the Martyrdom of Foreigners and Chinese Christians* (Edinburgh and London: Oliphant Anderson and Ferrier, 1903), p. 42.

9   A. Sowerby, quoted in R.C. Forsyth, *The China Martyrs of 1900* (London: The Religious Tract Society, 1904), p. 448.

10 Quotes this paragraph taken from letter from H. Dixon to A.H. Baynes, Taiyuan, 23 November 1885, quoted in 'Tidings from Shansi', *The Missionary Herald*, 1 August 1886, pp. 359,360.

11

Conflict and Encouragement

'We are often cast down by the manifold difficulties of the work
. . . if only the Spirit of God would work mightily.'
Joshua J. Turner, 1886[1]

'*Dui niu tan qin* . . . It means to play a lute to a cow.'

'Why would anyone do that?'

'It is a story. Let me enlighten you. A great musician, Gong, was walking in the countryside when he came across a cow in a field. Gong was a master of the *zheng*, a beautiful instrument played on strings of silk. Inspired by the beauty of the scene he sat down and began to play. The cow took no notice of him or his music. Gong played on, intoxicated with the exquisite richness of his music. When he finished he found the cow still eating grass.'

'So?'

'It is an idiom. We use it when someone speaks in a way that his audience cannot comprehend.'

Herbert and Elizabeth's teacher may have had his pupils in mind. There were thousands of these four character phrases dropped effortlessly into even the most casual of conversations; all seemingly meaningless but each one conveying some strand of ancient wisdom drawn from a fable.

'*Shou zhu dai tu.* This is another idiom. Protect a tree and await a hare.'

More incomprehension.

'A farmer was in his field and watched as a hare ran into a tree stump. The hare stopped dead. Very dead. The farmer was delighted and took the hare home for his supper. The next day he sat by the tree and waited for another hare to come along. And the next. And the next . . . until his farm was in ruins and he was very hungry . . . It means, as you say in England, there is no gain without pain.'

This was true of their study of Mandarin. Daily Herbert and Elizabeth twisted their tongues around strange sounds strung together to form sentences. Inflections of the voice, they learned, conveyed meaning, not emphasis as in English. The use of the wrong tone with the right sound brought incomprehension, offence or, more disconcerting, laughter. The written language – running left to right, or possibly right to left, or maybe top to bottom – was a mystifying mix of strange squiggles that must be memorized. They made their first attempts at Chinese calligraphy, grinding black ink from inksticks on flat stones to mix with water. Over time their first childish brush strokes slowly transformed to the precisely proportioned characters their teacher demanded.

The honeymoon was soon over, not only because of the difficulties of language learning but because Elizabeth fell ill. This was, no doubt, in part due to her pregnancy. She also succumbed to what Herbert attributed to his 'Congo fevers', carried, he believed, in his clothing to China. She was confined to bed for around two months and restricted in her opportunities to study, though she 'bravely pegs away', my great-grandfather reported. Herbert himself suffered in the hot summer rainy months. His memory 'played . . . sad pranks'2 and slowed his language learning to the point that he pleaded with his superiors in London for leniency in the examinations. Six years later, he still had not completed his studies to the satisfaction of the London office. Letters, which I find amusing to read, were exchanged. Herbert stubbornly appealed for an understanding of his situation; life was far too busy to do the exams he clearly had little intention of doing. The BMS, desperate to have one of their, by then, more senior China missionaries through his basic language programme, declared that he must show willing. The mission would reduce the requirements of the final examination if Herbert would just do it. He must define fifty characters selected at random from the New Testament and that would be that. I like to think he must have complied, sparing his superiors and himself further embarrassment, for the matter was not raised again.

As in the Congo, Herbert enjoyed success in his medical work, which he used as an opportunity to share the gospel with the ever-increasing numbers of patients and their families shown into his rooms by his servant. Despite having only one year's medical training, he seems to have had a natural ability at surgery. Given opportunity to practise his skills regularly, the complexity of the operations he undertook increased. An operation on a junior official was a noted success. The man sent a message announcing he would arrive in formal attire, accompanied by a band, and hand over a tablet declaring how superior Western skills were to those of his countrymen. Herbert declined this kind gesture, explaining that Elizabeth's ill health would not be helped by the noise. The official was not deterred. A carpenter arrived with the board and, amidst much hammering of nails and lighting of firecrackers, the inscription was hung above the front door of their home.

There were, my great-grandparents daily observed, three factors that devastated the people of Shanxi Province. Periodically and unpredictably, the fickle weather decimated the crops. Corruption in the brittle layers of local government was a second serious hardship. The greatest curse, however, was the deadly taste for 'foreign smoke'. Opium was grown in acre after acre of fertile fields. The drug's unmistakable sickly odour poisoned the air of every lane and alleyway in the city. Herbert encountered addict after addict, some as young as 15, their skin like parchment, slumped on pillows, drawing their addiction through wooden pipes three times a day. Whole families were wasted to the point of penury. Locally grown opium consumed a third of a worker's daily income, while the sticky brown paste imported from overseas was a luxury that ruined the rich.

Attempted opium suicides were not uncommon. A young man, having been berated by his stepmother for failing in his job, consumed an ounce of the drug. A junior wife, isolated by the senior wife, tried to take her own life through unhappiness. My great-grandfather encountered his first case on a scrap of waste ground. A beggar, in the tatters of his grimy clothing, had been thrown out under the scorching sun to die. Herbert's remedy was basic. He forced a tube down the man's throat and poured quart after quart of water into his stomach, flushing the contents out with a pump. He and his

Chinese servant worked for three hours until the heat became unbearable. They needed to get shelter for the man in a police watch-house nearby, but the resident policeman showed little interest in having the beggar on his territory. There was some bargaining to be done.

'You must pay the funeral expenses if he dies,' argued the policeman.

Herbert suspected the man could not be trusted and was capable of killing the beggar to keep the money for himself.

'I'll pay you the funeral fee . . . if he lives,' offered Herbert.

The deal was agreed and the beggar carried inside. When the stomach pump method failed to revive the man, Herbert experimented. He injected ammonia under the skin, a procedure he later described as 'so successful that I always use it in desperate cases'. It was, nevertheless, another four hours before the beggar was out of danger and the 'funeral expenses' handed over. My great-grandfather and his servant had spent the best part of a day saving the life of a man nobody cared about. In his first three years in China, Herbert saved the lives of thirty victims of opium. It was a time consuming commitment, requiring hours of patience, which took him away from his language study. He described it as 'a merely extraneous part of our work',[3] but he was aware that it brought relatives to his doors expressing their thanks, bringing credit to the mission in a way that their street preaching did not.

My great-grandfather's desire to use his medical skills to gain trust and opportunities to witness led to another clash with the BMS committee in London; this time about his ministry priorities. The mission questioned the usefulness of a visit to Shandong Province, a trip he used to improve his dental practice skills. It is not difficult to imagine Herbert's forthright response. The mission's secretary was subsequently at great pains to assure him that 'no sort of impression adverse'[4] to him lingered on. Tensions arose again two years later. The committee objected to Herbert opening a dispensary. Turner, Herbert's colleague in Xinzhou, undermined my great-grand-father's case, commenting that 'it is found impossible to mix the two things – preaching and medicine . . . I would rather see a man do one thing well than two things ill'.[5] The committee, while accepting that medical work was of value, laid out their views to Herbert in no uncertain terms: '. . . first be a Missionary, and secondly a medical man . . . the Committee will not allow the opening of the Dispensary, but ask you to give yourself thoroughly and primarily to Missionary work.'[6]

Herbert's determination to help the local people was not to be denied by a committee 5,000 miles away. He wrote again. He got his dispensary.

At the orphanage, Herbert had learned he needed to establish himself quickly; being 'heard' as well as seen was possibly the best way to survive. His outspokenness was not always a benefit. There were strong personalities on the mission field, and Christian love was sometimes buried beneath the weight of their opinions. In 1887, Timothy Richard was forced to leave Shanxi and came close to resignation. It was a chapter of the BMS's history in which my great-grandfather did not distinguish himself. When Herbert and Richard had first met in Taiyuan in 1886, there was already a palpable tension between the two men; an unease fostered in my great-grand-father by the hostile attitudes of Sowerby and Turner to Richard in his absence. Richard was not enamoured with

Herbert either. My great-grandfather had, in a letter unwisely published in *The Missionary Herald*, cast doubts on the effectiveness of Richard's six years of translation work and attempts to make Christianity attractive to the Chinese intellectual elite through education programmes. Richard, plainly upset, complained to the BMS about this new worker with 'some missionary experience in an uncivilized country'.[7] Herbert refused to back down. He wrote to his minister in London with a catalogue of Richard's failings. Richard's scheme to engage with China's literati was 'radically wrong'. Richard was accused of putting the work in Shandong Province in danger with his policies and his activities in Shanxi were questioned: 'The past work here is in my mind a failure being on wrong and eccentric lines'; '[the purchase of] four or five expensive machines that can give a spark of electricity or a lathe that costs a hundred pounds and then lies rusting and useless . . . point [Richard] out as quite unsuited for leader of a mission'; 'The only work worth anything has chiefly been done by Sowerby and Turner.'[8] Herbert's tirade against his senior missionary was unrelenting and unrepentant.

When Richard, seeking to make the gospel more culturally appropriate to the Chinese, used a white cross on a crimson background hung with yellow streamers 'exactly like those used in Buddhist temples', there was an outcry amongst his colleagues. His theology was denounced as 'a conglomerate teaching wherein Science, Heathenism, Roman Catholicism and Christianity are bundled up into a new "Gospel for the Nations"'. Only Evan Morgan supported his fellow Welshman. Sowerby, Turner, Herbert, and a new missionary, George Farthing, were adamant that something must be done to curb Richard's activities. Writing to the BMS, Herbert put his position succinctly: Richard should give up his 'peculiar views' or resign.[9] When Richard announced he would be leaving in the autumn of 1887, my great-grandfather was blunt enough to tell him to his face that he 'should be thankful to see him gone as his presence and influence cripples all evangelistic efforts in and around the city'.[10] [11]

It is doubtful that the mission's lack of success could be entirely attributed to the lack of unity in its missionaries' ranks or to Richard's influence in particular, but it was true that they had seen little progress in establishing a Shanxi church. While the work in Shandong prospered, the 'poor benighted heathens . . . full of fears of ghosts, demons, [and] dead men' of Shanxi failed to respond to the gospel in large numbers. Fifteen years after Richard first arrived in Taiyuan, there were only thirty-two church members, despite the efforts of eight men and their wives at various times. Herbert lamented that the work was slow, 'often dull and matter of fact'.[12]

Nevertheless, some of the Chinese believers proved to be outstanding evangelists and church leaders. Old He, aged over 60, was one of the first converts at the mission station in Xinzhou, and surrendered his interests in a dyeing business to become a poorly paid evangelist. When his employer offered him twice his salary to stay with the company, Old He would not be persuaded; he preferred 'God's work', he said. He was a quiet man and a capable evangelist. He introduced his younger cousin, an opium addict involved in trade on the Mongolian border, to Christ. Both were key workers in the mission's team of Chinese evangelists. Old He's courage made him an indomitable defender of Christians if they were under threat. He had been known to tackle a wolf armed only with a knife and had no fear of the authorities in the *yamen*. When his refusal to pay temple taxes landed him in court with the threat of a beating if he did not pay, he was undeterred. 'Jesus was crucified for me,' he told the missionaries, 'I can take a few blows for him.' It was a promise God would hold him to.

Another key member of the work at Xinzhou was an evangelist from Shandong. 'Little' Chao was by far the shortest of his colleagues but was perhaps the most significant Chinese partner in the ministry in Shanxi. Chao was a second generation Christian and a deacon in a church in Shandong. When he was accused of being a 'rice Christian', converted for his own material gain, Chao rejected the offer of a reward to betray the church. Timothy Richard had selected him as one of twelve evangelists he brought from Shandong to Shanxi, and Chao was now working alongside Turner.

The September 1889 edition of *The Missionary Herald*[13] contained a letter from Chao, highlighting the persecution of a small church about ten miles north-west of Xinzhou: 'The cause in Qicun greatly suffers persecution . . . Bad men curse us and even use weapons to hinder us from going to worship. We have borne their beatings but they grow worse daily. The officials have done nothing. These men are set on not allowing the preaching of the gospel at Qicun.' Chao's example of the persecution of Chinese Christians was not a rare occurrence. Chao had faced angry mobs. Old He had been badly treated by his employer and ex-workmates. One of the evangelists converted by Old He had been arrested and beaten for preaching, before being dragged unceremoniously out into the street where he jumped to his feet and began preaching again. The locals described the Christians as 'a nail in the eye' and, because they mixed with the *yang guizi*, 'foreign devils', labelled them 'secondary devils'. Chao's letter ended with a plea, 'I do not know what to do. I beg Pastor to hasten here for fear that further patience will result in loss of life.'

When Turner received the letter from Chao, some months before its publication in *The Missionary Herald*, he and Herbert had set out on horseback from Taiyuan to Qicun. Having stopped at Xinzhou to consult with the local Christians on what to do, they arrived in the town at nightfall a few days later and quickly became objects of curiosity. Several hundred people crowded into the courtyard of their lodgings, removed the windows by licking the paper with their tongues, and stared in on them until the missionaries blew out their candle to sleep.

The next day Herbert and Turner found a preaching spot on the streets. When a 'stout bully of a fellow' began to heckle Turner, my great-grandfather dropped his hand quietly onto the man's shoulder.

'You are a man of letters?' asked Herbert politely.

The man spun around and declared that he was not.

'I thought that was the case,' said Herbert.

The crowd laughed at Herbert's quick-witted retort. The man, by admitting to his own lack of education, had lost face with Turner's audience and he was reduced to silence. For five days the two missionaries were able to preach and hand out medicines without opposition.

My great-grandfather was away for a week and a half. He treated over three hundred patients and preached in Xinzhou and the surrounding villages. It was, he wrote, 'ten of the

happiest days I have spent in Shanxi'. He returned to his
home in Taiyuan with a desire to move north permanently.
The Turners were returning to Britain, leaving the station
without a missionary. Herbert had found a suitable, though
small, home for Elizabeth and their growing family. Benjamin
had been born in January 1886, Charlie twenty-one months
later, and Elizabeth was pregnant with a daughter, Mary. The
rent was £10 per year, payable in strings of 15,000 copper
coins weighing four or five hundredweight each quarter! As
to the visit to Qicun, Herbert was particularly cheery about
what he and Turner had achieved through their preaching
and medical work in persuading the local people that Christians could make a positive contribution to their lives. 'Thus
has the devil over-reached himself again; his opposition has
advertised us,' he wrote to the BMS, 'all has turned out for
the furtherance of the Gospel.'

NOTES

[1] Letter from J.J. Turner to the BMS, Xinzhou, undated, quoted
    in the BMS 94th Annual Report, 1886, p. 33.
[2] Quotes taken from letter from H. Dixon to A.H. Baynes,
    Taiyuan, 23 November 1885, quoted in 'Tidings from Shansi',
    The Missionary Herald, 1 August 1886.
[3] Quotes this paragraph taken from letter from H. Dixon to
    A.H. Baynes, Taiyuan, undated, quoted in 'Opium Poisoning
    Cases in North China', *The Missionary Herald*, 1 April 1889, p.
    134,135.
[4] Letter from A.H. Baynes to H. Dixon, London, 2 November 1888.
[5] J.J. Turner, quoted in letter from E.B. Underhill to H. Dixon,

London, 20 March 1890.

6   Letter from E.B. Underhill to H. Dixon, London, 20 March 1890.

7   T. Richard, 12 May 1887, quoted in B. Stanley, *The History of the BMS 1792–1992* (Edinburgh: T & T Clark, 1992), p. 190. Used with permission: B. Stanley.

8   Adapted from letter from H. Dixon to T.V. Tymms, Taiyuan, 18 March 1887.

9   Letter from H. Dixon to A.H. Baynes, Taiyuan, 25 April 1887.

10 Letter from H. Dixon to A.H. Baynes, Taiyuan, 14 October 1887.

11 Richard was a complex, autocratic character and the dispute multifaceted, by no means simply a quarrel between Richard and Herbert. Richard finally settled in Shanghai, working as an editor of Christian literature and garnering substantial influence, while remaining a BMS missionary. His views, much decried by some of his colleagues, gained prominence and helped to shape the direction of China's reform following the revolution in 1911 and the overthrow of China's last dynasty.

12   Letter from H. Dixon to A.H. Baynes, Taiyuan, 23 November 1885, quoted in 'Tidings from Shansi', *The Missionary Herald*, 1 August 1886, p. 361.

13 Quoted material below adapted from letter from H. Dixon to A.H. Baynes, Taiyuan, 1 May 1889, quoted in 'Mission Work in North China', *The Missionary Herald*, 1 September 1889, pp. 340–343.

12

Blessings in a Dark Land

'You will think writing all this is very much like boasting – no, dear Aunt, it is not written in such a spirit but just to let you know how the Lord has showered upon us temporal blessings in this dark dark [sic] land where there is so much to dishearten one.'

Elizabeth Dixon, 1889

There are few surviving letters written by my great-grand-mother. Missionary wives rarely had their views and reports of their ministry published in the pages of *The Missionary Herald*. It is, therefore, difficult for me to fully share the joys and worries that Elizabeth experienced in raising a family in China. There is one letter, however, that provides an understanding of her lifestyle, written just after the family moved from Taiyuan to Xinzhou. In December 1889, while settling into her new home, my great-grandmother came across a letter from an aunt living close to St David's. She had received it five years earlier while still in London and presumably meant to reply once in China. Establishing a home, language learning, illness, and the care of Benjie, Charlie and Mary had occupied her time. As Christmas approached, she finally took an opportunity to write back. It was January before she was able to finish her reply.

Elizabeth's letter is handwritten over seven pages and is full of her news. She was sad to have left their 'comfortable home in Taiyuan . . . where my three dear children were born'. Charlie, aged 2, had broken his leg. Herbert had performed surgery on it and she was confident that the bone would heal perfectly. Mary had been only a month and two days old when the family had embarked on the two-day journey north. It must have been a taxing ride with three small children. They would almost certainly have travelled in a small, covered, springless cart pulled by mules. The vehicle would have screeched hideously for the want of oil with every roll of its wheels through the Pass of Ten Mountain Ranges and along miles of stony river bed until finally they arrived at the city.

Xinzhou stands at the south-west entrance to one of Shanxi's great plains. It is guarded by hills on three sides and built on the slopes of a small rise. In the late 1800s it was a smaller version of Taiyuan and equally well fortified. The city's three and a half miles of brown-yellow earthwork walls were 50 feet high and 10 feet thick. For good measure the walls were protected by a 20 foot-deep moat, faced with brick and topped with battlements. Above the city gates towered imposing tiered pagodas, one at each point of the compass. On their arrival the family passed under the arch of an outer gate into a high-walled chamber before turning in through a second gate. The design was deliberate. The Chinese believed that evil spirits only travelled in straight lines and therefore would be caught in the chamber before they entered the city. Beyond the inner gate, Xinzhou's main streets were busy with mules and camels carrying tea to Russia, and bringing felt and furs back to her markets. The priorities of the city's 1,800 families were soon evident. There were six residences for officials, seven schools, eight large opium stores and more than seventy opium dens.

Elizabeth's three servants, who moved with her from Taiyuan, were already well schooled in Elizabeth's domestic pride as she set about creating a new home for the family. She had become renowned for her cleanliness, and her kitchen was described as the cleanest in China. Xinzhou posed fresh challenges. The city was beset by sand storms, severe enough to reduce visibility to a few metres, which layered everything in deposits of uninvited gritty dust. The place was also infested with rats. Local poisons had little effect on the vermin and there was no respite from them day or night. The ceilings of the house were constructed with three thicknesses of wet paper, stretched on a wood framework and whitewashed from wall to wall. When dry, the paper became as tight as a skin on a drum, which formed a perfect playground for the rats to tumble around on, keeping the household awake. The best counsel of Xinzhou residents was to leave them alone. 'If you don't annoy them, they will not hurt you, but if you try to kill them, they will increase more and more, and come at night and eat up your clothes, and perhaps bite you when you are asleep, so you had better have nothing to do with them'[1] was the unhelpful advice Elizabeth received.

One of the servants was designated to do the house-hold chores, dusting and polishing, trimming the lamps and setting the table, while the cook doubled as the clothes washer. The indispensable role of gatekeeper was assigned to the man who cared for the cow, calf and ponies and kept the house fires burning through the winter. Elizabeth also hired a children's nurse, an elderly widow, who tottered around after my great-grandmother on her 3-inch long, bound feet, trying to learn the idiosyncrasies of the foreigners.

Elizabeth's upbringing in the kitchen at St David's was not wasted in China. Despite having lived in Shanxi for over four years, she and Herbert had no stomach for Chinese cuisine and she had trained the cook to serve British recipes. A market held every other day provided vegetables, grain, fruit and eggs. Mutton and beef were cheap and there was chicken, duck and pheasant to buy. Herbert's patients often brought gifts of food in lieu of payment for their treatment. Grapes were a penny a pound throughout the year, and the market also sold apricots, apples, peaches and plums. When fruit was in season Elizabeth boiled it up to make jam. She used baking powder to make bread and shook cream in a large bottle to make butter.

If Elizabeth's day to day labours went unmentioned in the lengthy reports Herbert sent to the BMS for publication in *The Missionary Herald*, it took an amusing article of a 'Dr Ashmore of China' to highlight for readers in Britain the daily, essential industry of the mission's women. The doctor informed readers of the June 1891 edition:

She is the general supplemer of all manner of minor unfinished items in the round of missionary life. She mixes medicines, spreads plasters, gives out doses of painkiller, warns the children against green fruit and colic, puts on patches, sews on buttons, deals out bits of thread and needles, asks the children how their mothers are and the mothers how their children are, keeps count of baptizing gowns, looks after the preparation for communion service, keeps the desk supplied with postage stamps . . . and so on, with twenty other things of no great account in making up a 'report', but all of which are valuable items of solid missionary usefulness.

The doctor was also not above making fun of the missionary husbands, who compiled their reports of great account:

> Ostensibly, the husband is here to do a little civilising, as a sort of secondary work . . . but his wife often has to keep her eye on him to prevent his being barbarized while he is about it. He would go round with sleeves out at the elbows, and shoes careened over on one side. He would get to taking his breakfast in the pantry or on his writing-desk. His wife has . . . to make him presentable and a credit to the Missionary Union that sent him out . . . tells him where he left his hat when he cannot find it, reminds him that his coat has not been brushed nor his shoes blacked when he is going to make a call . . . Some of them would starve if their good wives did not look after them.[2]

Well fed and suitably spruce, my great-grandfather quickly established himself in Turner's place in Xinzhou.[3] Despite his reassurances to the BMS committee of the priority of preaching, it was frequently his medical work that demanded his time. His sermon notes point to his practical view of ministry: 'Christ . . . has taught us to feed the hungry, clothe the naked, comfort the sick . . . To conquer the world for Christ by love, that is Christ's will.' Herbert was in constant demand, whether working in the small mission hospital established in the city, or on frequent visits to surrounding villages. The hospital, a suite of five rooms and a kitchen adjacent to the Xinzhou chapel, accommodated ten patients on brick beds. Pots and pans were lent to friends who accompanied the patients, so that they could provide meals for them. Herbert had a varied catalogue of ailments to deal with: cataracts and carbuncles, diseases of the hips and spine, gunshot wounds and injuries from violent fights, as well as tending the opium addicts who sought his help. Droughts caused diphtheria, measles, scarlet fever and typhus, and the floods that followed brought cholera and dysentery.

This approach to mission had its advantages. His hospital patients were required to attend Sunday services and morning and evening prayers, as well as getting regular instruction from an elderly Chinese evangelist. Herbert was not above sending stories of his successes back to Britain to bolster his case for sending out missionaries with medical skills. His treatments provided opportunities for witness and enhanced the reputation of the mission. 'Could you but know the wild rumours afloat as to what horrible practices we indulge in during worship, and the dread there often is at the thought of entering our chapel,' he wrote, 'you would the better appreciate the use of our hospital in teaching the people what is meant by worship and prayer . . . Again and again do I hear the remark as I ride out, "Oh, he is going to see the sick"; and curses die on their lips as they see our practical religion in our medical work.'[4]

Turner had found it hard to get established in Xinzhou. The mission premises were not in a prominent location. Landlords were reluctant to rent him a shop on the main street in which to sell literature and hold meetings. Turner was frustrated by the lack of interest the local people showed in even their own religion, let alone Christianity. They only seemed interested in money; a province of bankers, businessmen and pawnshop owners, who, it was said, were 'misers, preferring money to life'.[5] In 1886, two converts, one of them Old He, had been baptized and a church established. By the time Herbert and Elizabeth arrived three years later, the congregation had grown to more than thirty but of these no more than ten were members and church attendance was dependent on the weather.

The nearby market town of Qicun proved more fruitful. Four Chinese evangelists, supported in part by local Christians, were active in the church, and new converts joined them to preach on the streets in small groups. Herbert held meetings there for large numbers of inquirers, started a school and tried to establish a Sunday school. The Qicun church numbered twenty when my great-grandparents set up their home in Xinzhou. Within three months it had grown to thirty, and a year later the congregation was 100.

Progress, however, was hampered by persecution. In Qicun, whenever the Christians met for prayers or services, stone-throwing became the 'fashionable evening amusement' of local troublemakers. Zhou, one of the church leaders, came under threat. A cousin vowed that the coffin of Zhou's ailing mother would not leave the house until Zhou made offerings to the idols in accordance with the temple's customs. Zhou refused. When a crowd attacked the mission, an elderly member of the congregation was beaten up. Herbert intervened on the Christians' behalf, but when Zhou's mother died the tension in the town escalated. Zhou came under more pressure to go to the temple and his cousin threatened to kill him. Herbert went to the local magistrate and was able to secure a warrant for the cousin's arrest. Finding Zhou's cousin in a barber's shop, the town elders informed the barber that he need not shave his customer as 'his Worship the Magistrate has just sent a pressing invitation for him to meet him'.[6] They then hauled him off to court. Free from further opposition, Zhou was able to give his mother a Christian burial watched by 200 onlookers. Nevertheless, it was weeks before the cousin finally gave up his vow to kill Zhou. He kowtowed in acknowledgement of his crimes and handed Herbert his knife. My great-grandfather, for some curious reason, saw fit to hang it in his study above a picture of the Reverend Richard Glover, chairman of the BMS China subcommittee.

Elizabeth's care for the children and upkeep of the home meant she could not be fully involved in the medical work. She dressed the wounds of women patients and administered chloroform when Herbert performed operations. Like her father, she had a love of hymns and taught the Chinese evangelists songs which she and Herbert had translated into Chinese. Despite the limitations of her involvement, she and my great-grandfather believed they were in this mission as a family. The witness of their daily lives was an essential contribution to their ministry. Elizabeth and the children sometimes travelled out into the countryside with Herbert. These journeys were not without risk. There was little to guarantee that they would be well received. Herbert often had doors slammed in his face, and foul language shouted from open shop fronts followed him along streets. Rumours about the barbaric practices of 'foreign devils' were rife. In taking the children with them, he and my great-grandmother hoped that these prejudices could be broken down.

Elizabeth's ability to be involved in ministry was also hampered by her health. She was often unwell. In 1891, she gave birth to her fourth child in five years – a third boy, Ridley. A BMS deputation, which visited them that year, was concerned enough to devote a whole paragraph to her in their report. They requested that the BMS provide two lady missionaries to join her in Xinzhou, 'where Mrs Dixon – two days' journey from any Englishwoman, and in delicate health – has a life and work of the loneliest kind'.[7] Her isolation was exacerbated by the Chinese view of women. Women, society decreed, were inferior to men, being as far below the male sex as the earth was beneath the sky. A married woman was a slave in her own house, and could be sold in times of poverty as readily as a piece of furniture. Women were not to be seen on the streets of Xinzhou. Whenever Elizabeth wished to go out into the city she must summon a sedan chair and be ferried behind curtains to her destination and back.

The situation Chinese women faced and the difficulties that the BMS missionaries had in attracting them to their meetings were not ignored. There were strong calls to allow single women to join the mission in China and take up the challenges of educating girls, providing medical help for women, and training Chinese women to go into homes and share the gospel with Chinese wives. The London committee demurred, fearing that Chinese bias against women would hinder the mission's work, and they would not sanction the sending of single women. The BMS deputation disagreed, believing that single women would be 'free from family cares' and could 'prosecute a work amongst the women as effectively as the brethren are doing amongst the men'.[8] Herbert pressed the case. The China Inland Mission, also working in Shanxi, was successfully using single women to build up a congregation of fifty or more Chinese women, whereas the BMS missionaries had failed to attract a single one. Regrettably, when the BMS agreed to the appointing of four women from the Baptist Zenana Mission,[9] a sister organization, they were sent to Shandong Province. Elizabeth's need of help was ignored.

My great-grandmother did not necessarily share the deputation's concerns over her health. Her troubles pushed her closer to God. 'I have realized His presence more . . . than I have ever done in my life. He has heaped blessings upon us ever since we came to this dark land', she wrote to one of her aunts. Herbert, however, had real concerns over her health. Elizabeth was suffering with serious fainting fits. She caught cholera and, although she recovered, she was left 'much pulled down in strength'.[10]

By 1893, Herbert and Elizabeth had been in China for eight years and were due under the provisions of the BMS to return to Britain within the next year for a break from the demands of their work. They had intended to work in Xinzhou for another two to three years, but Elizabeth's health deteriorated to the point that Herbert, perhaps remembering his own experience in the Congo, had to act. He did not wait for permission to leave China. He booked berths on a steamer bound for Vancouver and the family hurried south to Shanghai, leaving the work at Xinzhou in the hands of Chao and the other Chinese evangelists. On 6 May, my great-grandparents and the children boarded a Canadian Pacific Royal Mail steamship, the white-hulled *Empress of India*. Six months later, when the P&O ship *Rosetta* steamed into Shanghai harbour, Herbert was among the passengers. Elizabeth was not; she had remained behind in England with Benjie, Charlie, Mary and Ridley. It would be four years before she and Herbert were reunited.

NOTES

[1] Quoted in J.J. Turner, 'New Work in North China', *The Missionary Herald*, 1 March 1886, p. 85.

[2] 'Dr Ashmore of China', 'The Wives of Missionaries', *The Missionary Herald*, 1 June 1891, p. 253.

[3] Turner did return to Xinzhou in 1891 for approximately one year, but ill health forced him to return to Britain.

[4] Letter from H. Dixon to the BMS, Xinzhou, undated, quoted in 'Mr. and Mrs. Herbert Dixon and Family', *The Missionary Herald*, 1 December 1890, pp. 433,435.

[5] Chinese opinion, quoted in H.R. Williamson, *British Baptists in China 1845–1952*, p. 49.

[6] Quotes this paragraph taken from letter from H. Dixon to A.H. Baynes, Xinzhou, 13 March 1890, quoted in 'Tidings from North China', *The Missionary Herald*, 1 September 1890, pp. 333,335.

[7] R. Glover and T.M. Morris, 'China – Report of the Recent Deputation', *The Missionary Herald*, 1 May 1892, p. 201.

[8] Ibid.

[9] The 'Ladies' Association for the Support of Zenana Work and Biblewomen in India, in connection with the Baptist Mission-

ary Society' was formed in 1869. The name was derived from work in India among women living in *zenanas*, Hindu dwellings for high-caste women from which males, other than family members, were excluded. The name Baptist Zenana Mission was adopted in 1897.

10   Letter from H. Dixon to A.H. Baynes, Xinzhou, undated, quoted in 'Cheering News from Shansi', *The Missionary Herald*, 1 December 1892, p. 480.

13

Cambridge – Apart for a While

'Conscientious people are apt to see their duty in that which is the most painful course.'

George Eliot, 1860[1]

There were four great partings in Elizabeth and Herbert's lives. The first came when they were engaged and Herbert sailed for the Congo, leaving his fiancée behind in Britain. This second parting was twelve years later. Caught between his passion to take the gospel to the unreached and his love for his dear wife and children, he took the decision made by many other Victorian missionary men faced with the same dilemma. He would return alone. My grandfather was 8 years old and needing a good education. Elizabeth required better medical care than Herbert could provide. They had entered the mission with their eyes open; separation was part of the sacrifice that all missionaries were expected to be willing to make.

Herbert's decision was, in part, also a response to a shift in emphasis of the BMS's work in China. A ready-made congregation of thirty Chinese believers, driven west by floods and famine in Shandong, had settled in Shaanxi Province (which neighbours Shanxi), creating a Christian community north of the provincial capital, Xian. The work in Shandong was proving fruitful, its thirteen missionaries nurturing over one thousand Chinese Christians. However, with seven missionaries, Shanxi could boast no more than around thirty Christians, a membership roughly equal to the fledgling Shaanxi church. In addition, the quarrel with Timothy Richard six years before had left the Shanxi missionary force with ongoing tensions between those who supported Richard and those who didn't. The missionary team in Shanxi was depleted from seven men to four as supporters of Richard moved to Shaanxi. Herbert's absence put his colleagues under even greater strain. He had purchased a return ticket in China, and had every intention of using it as soon as the BMS sanctioned his plans. After a lengthy interview, the China Committee deemed 'it right that he should return at the earliest practicable moment . . . in accordance with his own strong desire'.[2]

The good 'Dr Ashmore of China' was not wrong in his assessment of the predicament of the missionary man if he did not have his wife to care for him. Herbert was troubled by an assortment of difficulties. The Shanxi summer rains made roads into impassable morasses and he could not get out as much as he would have liked. He was feeling under the weather, suffering with aches and pains and headaches. He had rheumatism, he said, in his shoulder. One of the two pear trees he had planted in a village outside of Xinzhou had died and the second looked destined to follow it. He was frustrated that all of his fortnightly letters to Elizabeth since his arrival back in China had failed to be delivered. One of Elizabeth's letters had obviously spent part of its journey in water and was open. Her envelopes were of poor quality. It was clear she had not added the full amount of stamps. Money was tight and he had been forced to pay excess postage since there was only 3½ pennies-worth on the envelope. Herbert could not be bothered with variety in his diet, and had been reduced to eating tinned salmon. Elizabeth had apparently forgotten his birthday . . .

Nevertheless, apart from these ordeals, my great-grand-father held onto his optimistic outlook. 'Amid a good deal to try and depress me', he informed Elizabeth, 'I have found great comfort in looking up and knowing God will never leave me nor forsake me.'

Herbert's letters to Elizabeth during their separation are full of Victorian husbandly advice on buying a feather bed, keeping newspapers out of Benjie's reach as 'unsuitable for the boy to read', and buying a double porridge pot. He wryly commented on Elizabeth's ambitious use of the term 'drawing room' to describe their small sitting room. Intriguingly, he added that she should 'dress as your conscience dictates, and apologize to no one'.

My great-grandmother was not having an easy time, either. She too was suffering with rheumatism and there were diffi-culties in her Welsh family to deal with. In the spring of 1894, her father was ill. He had lost his appetite and complained of a bad stomach. After a brief period of illness, Thomas Williams died and Elizabeth's family was reduced to just two siblings, herself and John, plus her adopted brother, Eben-ezer. Both her mother and her brother George had died while she had been in China. I am sure Elizabeth saw God's hand in her being in England when Thomas passed away. She travelled to Wales for the funeral but, for reasons not revealed in her letters, John snubbed her. Ebenezer did not even bother to come, a matter of sufficient scandal to be reported in the Pembrokeshire press.

Elizabeth and the children found accommodation in Cambridge, where they were taken under the wing of Charles Foster and his wife, Jane. These friends of the Dixon family were people of considerable affluence. Foster's grandfather, a mayor of Cambridge, had founded a bank in the town centre and the family owned farms, mills and property, including Anstey Hall, a mansion on the outskirts of the city. The family's nonconformist sympathies were also strong; Foster was descended from a family of six brothers who had been close friends of John Bunyan. Jane sent Elizabeth flowers and magazines, and bought sweets for Benjie, Charlie, Mary and Ridley. Jane's daughter also took Elizabeth out in her carriage from time to time. Foster had a reputation for plain speaking and, no doubt, found a like-minded man in my great-grandfather. The family's largesse was also valuable to Herbert's work in Xinzhou. Foster sponsored Old He's ministry at Qicun and provided the finance to initiate new work in another of the outlying villages.

In Herbert's absence, Chao, Old He and their Chinese colleagues proved good workers, pushing the work forward rather than simply maintaining it. Herbert was delighted to see noticeable development in one of their newer ventures, an attempt to establish Christian schools. Their first school in Xinzhou had failed for the want of a suitable teacher. It was, as Herbert noted, impossible to '"create" Christian teachers'[3] and the use of non-believers would not be contemplated. A second school, founded under pressure from Christian parents loath to send their children to schools where they must worship Wen Chang, the Taoist god of literature, was more successful. A Mr Tong, an elderly teacher, had been found to tutor four boys, one of whom was quickly dismissed because of his refusal to learn. The school struggled on until the end of the year, when parents realized that Tong's students had learned more in one year than pupils in other schools had managed in three. Suddenly, there were sixteen students enrolled and, while pupil numbers had subsequently fallen, the Xinzhou school was firmly established.

The school at Qicun had also struggled into existence. Opposition was fierce. There were malicious rumours that Christians were engaged in child stealing and harvesting the eyes and hearts of the pupils for their own evil purposes. The school had, nevertheless, grown to ten pupils, and some of the boys had become Christians. When Herbert visited, he found the children sitting on long benches at rough wooden tables in their smock jackets and ankle-length trousers. Some were earnestly copying out characters with coarse ink brushes while others recited aloud the passage they had learned that day. The classroom was full of noise, each student shouting above the others to make themself heard, or the whole group combining into raucous sing-song chanting of a passage. In total there were forty to fifty pupils now enrolled in the mission's schools, and at Qicun two or three girls had begun to attend classes. The Chinese Christians were ambitious. They proposed to start two new schools in other villages, where they would also pay a quarter of the teachers' salaries.

The success of the mission schools had not, however, won the majority of the population over to accept Christianity as beneficial to the community. The Shanxi church was never free from persecution. In one area, unrest flared up when a believer refused to pay the temple tax. Summoned to the temple to explain himself, he was thrown from a platform into the courtyard below and beaten. He was then dragged down to a river where one of his assailants threatened to smash his head with a boulder. When a local official interceded, the man was hauled back to the temple, tied up and told that he would starve to death if he didn't pay. My great-grandfather was called upon to intervene. His appeals to the magistrate forced the temple authorities to back down, and the man was struck from the temple's books. However, six other members of the mission's meetings then refused to pay, aggravating the situation further and creating more tensions for Herbert to deal with.

Despite the violent opposition, there was growth in the church. While congregations fluctuated in number quite dramatically at times, the Shanxi church began to emerge as a visible presence of committed believers in the province's towns and villages. In 1896, while the citizens of Taiyuan welcomed the Chinese New Year of the Monkey with processions of dragon parades, endless barrages of firecrackers and raucous circles of gambling, another noteworthy event, which Sowerby floridly described as sending 'a thrill of holy gladness through the sympathetic angel hosts above',[4] was being held in the city. It was a conference for Shanxi Christians; not one in which the missionaries took pre-eminence with discussions in English, but the first gathering of Shanxi's indigenous church conducted in Chinese. Three hundred Chinese Christians, men and women, congregated in the chapel of the Schofield Memorial Hospital. Down the centre of the chapel ran a wooden screen, the men sitting on benches on one side, the women squatting on a brick platform on the other. Hymns were sung to the accompaniment of an American organ, and the topics for discussion ranged from foot binding to persecution, and from self-support to the second coming. Certain Chinese leaders, among them Chao, were remarkably eloquent as they expounded their views and led discussions. Others came with a miscellany of dialects, mispronounced vowels, and misplaced consonants. Sowerby noted humorously that their speech gave the impression of ill-planned mouths, full of loose tongues and teeth jumbled together. The conference proved a success. The Chinese Christians returned to their homes with an understanding that they were not a few isolated and persecuted believers in remote locations, but identified with a significant congregation.

By late 1897, when Herbert once again returned to Britain, the ministry had developed considerably under his and Chao's leadership. In Xinzhou there were regular Sunday services attended by men and women, a Thursday evening singing class, a prayer meeting on Saturday nights, and Bible classes throughout the week. They had started a well-regarded day school that had spawned a Sunday school. A Christian bookshop on the main street was attracting good custom. The medical work continued through the hospital, the dispensary and my great-grandfather's tours of the countryside. Herbert listed mission stations at six centres, some employing a full-time evangelist and becoming financially independent of the

Xinzhou church. There also appeared to have been a marked improvement in relationships with the local population. In the autumn before he left China, nineteen people were baptized.

This time Herbert's departure did not leave the Xinzhou church bereft of a missionary. His isolation had ended the year before, when he was joined by a Scottish recruit, Reverend Adam McCurrach, who settled down to learn Mandarin. In Herbert's absence, McCurrach was joined by Sowerby. In Taiyuan, George Farthing, well established as a senior missionary with eleven years' experience, assumed Sowerby's responsibilities. Farthing had the assistance of another probationer, Tom Underwood. Underwood, formerly a gentleman's outfitter, had travelled out with McCurrach, both of them leaving their fiancées behind in Britain.

I have no detail of my great-grandparents' reunion. In the story of a lifetime, the period Herbert spent in England with his children was brief, just fourteen months. While her husband toured churches and harried the BMS and Zenana committees to agree to send single women to work in Shanxi, Elizabeth set about preparing herself, Benjie, Charlie, Mary and Ridley for another parting; the third of their lives – this time, not from each other but from the children. She and Herbert were leaving for China. The children were staying behind. Four separate guardians were found, one for each child. The boys were enrolled at the London Missionary Society's School for the Sons of Missionaries at Blackheath in London. Mary was registered at Walthamstow Hall, the sister school in Sevenoaks, Kent.

Before my great-grandparents left for China, the family posed for two photographs that I have in my collection. The first shows Elizabeth, in a full-length appliquéd dress sewn with large flowers along the sleeves and down the bodice, with Ridley, now aged 7, on her right, pressing himself into the picture. Herbert, in dark bow tie, suit and waistcoat, his beard and moustache neatly trimmed, stands suitably upright at the back, his arm around Charlie's shoulder, with Benjie and Mary seated around him. The boys have outfits of stiff white collars, light bow ties and suits to match their father's, their hair impeccably parted on the left. Mary has a velvet dress with a lace collar and cuffs, and holds a book. All of them wear appropriately austere expressions as befits a formal Victorian family portrait. The second picture is less posed. The composition has slipped, revealing their close- ness. Herbert holds Mary's hand across his lap. Ridley leans against his mother, his fingers entwined in hers. Benjie has taken Herbert's place at the back, holding Charlie close. My great-grandfather sits to the left, my great-grandmother on the right, together enfolding their children into the picture frame.

In the early afternoon, on Saturday, 11 February 1899, Elizabeth and Herbert boarded *RMS Scot* in the rain at Southampton, heading for Cape Town, en route to Xinzhou. Their separation from the children had come two days earlier. This third major parting in my great-grandparents' lives must have been a very bitter moment. But as they released Benjie, Charlie, Mary and Ridley to their guardians they did not know that this parting was to be, for the children, the final parting.

NOTES

[1] George Eliot, *The Mill on the Floss* (Edinburgh and London: Blackwood, 1860), ch. 5.

[2] Minutes of the BMS China Committee, 18 July 1893.

[3] Letter from H. Dixon to the BMS, Shansi, undated, quoted in 'Hsin Cheo', *The Missionary Herald*, 1 May 1894, p. 197.

[4] A. Sowerby, 'Conference of Chinese Christians in Shanxi', *The Missionary Herald*, 1 July 1896, p. 364.

14

Towards Journey's End

'The Chinese had no idea of the various countries which composed the world; their idea was that there was one vast middle kingdom as they call it, represented by a huge circle. That was China, of course. The circle was fitted in a square, and the four empty spaces at the corners of the square where the circle did not touch, and which embraced all the rest of the world, was occupied by one kingdom, which they called "The Kingdom of the Foreign Devils."'

Charles T. Studd, 1893[1]

In the late nineteenth century, the equations of distance and time were rapidly being transformed. Technology – the telegraph, telephone and transport – was shrinking the circumference of the world. A button pressed in London propelled a message to Tehran inside two minutes. The telephone was rapidly gaining in popularity as a means of instant communication. *RMS Scot*, Elizabeth and Herbert's ship, had broken a world record. Six years before their voyage to the Far East, powered by coal-fired engines and blasting steam from its tall twin funnels, the ship had coasted from its dock in England to Cape Town in under fifteen days. On their return to Xinzhou, my great-grandparents were able to take a train along a new railway from Tianjin on the coast to the Hebei town of Baoding. A journey of 150 miles was completed in a day. This was a considerably shorter time than the tedious five or six days' expedition needed for travelling by river boat.

These advances presented a huge challenge to an ancient mindset of the Chinese. China's equations of introspective superiority were being put to the test. Their concept of 'The Kingdom of the Foreign Devils', compressed into the margins of their maps with little distinction between nationalities, was being invaded with new ideas. The globe in Herbert's Xinzhou book room was a fascination to passers-by because it was so alien to their own view of the earth.

The differing perceptions of Westerners and Chinese underpinned another growing tension within China. Resentment over the presence of privileged foreigners in their country was intensifying amongst the rural poor in the areas south of Beijing and Tianjin. Timothy Richard told a story which aptly illustrated the differences in perspective of the Chinese and the colonial interlopers. At dawn one day, as he was setting out from a Shandong village on horseback, he encountered the only other man on the street.

'Where do you come from?' asked the man.

'Qingzhou.'

'But you are not Chinese. You are a foreigner.'

'Yes, from England.'

'Hah, that country has rebelled against us.'

'England could never rebel,' replied Richard, 'she never belonged to China.'

His acquaintance reacted angrily. 'But she did! She paid tribute to China. When she rebelled, it was the greatest rebellion the earth has ever known . . .'[2]

As my great-grandparents set sail from Southampton, ill feelings such as this were about to degenerate into a turmoil of rebellion – the Boxer Rebellion.

Herbert and Elizabeth's journey from Britain to Xinzhou took them a leisurely five months. *RMS Scot*, at less than record-breaking speed, transported them through a violent storm and huge seas to Madeira. 'We were almost all of us in bed as sick as sick could be,' Herbert wrote to my grandfather. 'Tuesday we struggled into our clothes and got outside for an hour or so but heavy seas drove us all inside again. Wednesday a huge sea smashed a boat on the poop deck and almost drowned us out of the saloon. Cabins have been leaking – meals have been a misery – and it has been almost an impossibility to write a letter.'

From Madeira they sailed on down the coast of Africa through the calmer waters of the tropics. I wonder whether Herbert glimpsed the coast of Congo as they sailed past. I know that he maintained an interest in the ministry and the missionaries he had worked with. Although he was fully committed to the Chinese church, perhaps there were unspoken regrets that the work he had helped to start continued without him.

Finally, *RMS Scot* pitched and rolled around the Cape to her destination, Durban; a city with parades of colonnaded shops, lines of trams, a railway station and streets to match London. The ship sailed around a wooded bluff and into the narrow neck of the harbour entrance. Herbert and Elizabeth were lowered in a basket down the side of the ship to a waiting tug and ferried across to the quay, a cluster of warehouses built on the back of a broad sandbank. There Charles, Herbert's elder brother, was waiting for them. They had not seen each other for twenty-eight years.

Herbert's siblings and their families, presumably seizing what they believed to be an opportunity to build better lives for themselves, had settled about two hundred and fifty miles inland, on the wide flat stretches of undulating grassland of the Orange Free State. My great-grandparents spent nine weeks with Herbert's brothers, touring the state and taking a train to visit the gold mines at Johannesburg. Edwin lived in a small farming community. He was a local Justice of the Peace and ran a general store, in which he employed Charles. Close by, Oliver had acquired a 1,000 acre farm of goats, sheep and 'cattle and horses innumerable'. He owned a shop and a post office in a galvanized iron house which doubled as the farmhouse. Tragically, Herbert's eldest brother, Arthur, had drowned some years earlier.

At the end of their visit, Herbert and Elizabeth boarded a small, uncomfortable steamer, the *SS Umbilo*, for the three-week voyage across the Indian Ocean to Sri Lanka, and from there sailed to Singapore and on to Saigon, Hong Kong and Shanghai. Herbert thoroughly enjoyed himself – reading Christian biographies, playing chess, winning prizes at deck quoits, and shark fishing with a red and white rag as bait; activities he described in detail in his frequent letters to the children: 'We visited the Botanical Gardens [in Saigon] and saw . . . an elephant, tigers, leopards, monkeys, deer, a bear, snakes, iguanas . . . with nothing to pay. Among them was a perfectly black leopard. We thought Ridley especially would have enjoyed them.' Wherever he went he collected stamps to add to his son's albums, amongst them a blue penny Ceylon he bought for eight pennies, a Maritime Diamond Jubilee stamp which cost a shilling and an Old Transvaal four penny brown 'worth £2 now – so take good care of it'.

Elizabeth fared better on land than at sea. She was ill with another fainting fit, had a fever and suffered bouts of seasickness in rough seas. She became frustrated by delays when their boat to Colombo was becalmed with burst pipes and, not surprisingly, depressed after the death of two of the second-class passengers. The trips she took ashore, however, were enchanting. She had taken pleasure in walking the pebbled streets of Madeira, and enjoyed her visits to the Roman Catholic cathedral and the fish and fruit market, where the bananas and oranges proved dearer than she expected. Amused by the island's 'quaint' vehicles, she wrote to Benjie that they gave 'the impression of bedsteads on sledges as they went thump thump over the stones'. In South Africa she had relished picnics by the roadside, rides out in wagons pulled by teams of four or six horses, and 'mixing' with the Fengu, Sotho and Zulu Africans. Now she took great delight in their drives in a carriage through the cinnamon gardens of Colombo and along avenues of green shade in Saigon, where the trees that lined their route met overhead. In Shanghai she indulged herself, shopping for silk to send home.

My abiding impression from Elizabeth and Herbert's letters to their children is of a happy couple enjoying the adventure of middle age, free for the time being from the hardship of missionary service; a couple on their second honeymoon. Of course, they missed Benjie, Charlie, Mary and Ridley. 'We have often wished you were with us,' Elizabeth wrote to my grandfather, and Herbert was eager to remind him that he was not forgotten, 'I feel very near to you . . . for I can at any moment look up to God and know that he can see us both.' They were 'hungry' for letters from the children, and expressed their disappointment to find only one from Mary waiting for them in Durban. Elizabeth perhaps summed up her feelings best to her brother, Ebenezer.

> I could not help reflecting as we flew along the dusty streets [in Durban] how wonderful it seemed that I should have the privilege and pleasure of seeing so much of this beautiful world of ours. Oh, travelling is a great delight – apart from the great longing that comes over me at times for the sound of my darlings' voices. When I do think of them, I cannot but be thankful for the wonderful way in which God has guided us in arranging for them during our separation.

It was Sunday, 16 July before Herbert and Elizabeth approached the gates of Xinzhou on horseback. The final eleven days on the road from the railway station at Baoding had dissipated much of the enjoyment of their journey as they trudged along tracks churned to muddy rivers. A two-day thunderstorm delayed them at one of the inns, hurling 'hailstones like marbles' through the fragile paper windows. The inns were dirtier than Elizabeth remembered and Herbert was forced to put up camp beds beneath mosquito nets to avoid sleeping on the 'lively' brick *kangs* and to keep the flies at bay. Standing in the shade of the walls of a temple close to the city gates they found Old He, Chao and a group of Christians waiting to welcome them. Another company met them at the gates and, finally, Sowerby and McCurrach appeared to escort them back to the mission.

There were mixed blessings in their return. There was female companionship for Elizabeth. McCurrach was now married – his wife, Clara, a headmistress from a girls' school in Yorkshire, and Fanny, the wife of Tom Underwood in Taiyuan, had sailed to China together and the two couples married on the same day in Shanghai. The McCurrachs, however, were living in my great-grandparents' old home. For three months, Herbert and Elizabeth survived in the old mission courtyard, using the medical rooms as living quarters and eating with the Sowerbys, until they secured premises across the street in a house desperately needing renovation. Battalions of insects occupied every crack and corner. Two coffins were found in the living room; both contained the previous owner's deceased relatives! It was weeks before the workmen, having replaced ceilings and floors, finished the refurbishing. Elizabeth and Herbert moved in and my great-grandmother started to educate her new school of servants on how to get her home in order and prepare meals the way that she and my great-grandfather liked them.

There was an exciting sense of purpose about the Xinzhou mission. The impetus for growth Herbert had witnessed before returning to Britain had been maintained by the Sowerbys,

McCurrachs, Chao and the Chinese church leaders. The work had expanded to seven established centres in five county towns and two market towns. Each centre had a resident Chinese evangelist and Qicun, the strongest of these churches, was considering appointing its own Chinese pastor. In Xinzhou the chapel was too small to accommodate the growing congregation and there were two services each Sunday morning. Four dozen baptisms had been carried out, twenty-two of these just three weeks before Herbert and Elizabeth's arrival. One of the four ladies baptized was a woman in her sixties whose feet had been unbound recently. She had walked fifteen miles to Xinzhou.

'I walked a few steps and then stopped and prayed to Jesus; then walked a little way further and then stood and prayed again, and so the Lord helped me to do it; but in all my life I had never walked more than three miles before,' she told the missionaries.[3]

There was also good news of two missionaries coming to join the team. Herbert was particularly happy that one of them was 28-year-old Bessie Renaut, a single woman from east London sent by the Baptist Zenana Mission. On his return to Britain, Herbert had taken a letter from the Xinzhou church. The contents were wordy, but the point unambiguous:

There is a large increase of worshippers on the Sabbath, including both women and girls. These are warm-hearted believers in the Lord, but there is no lady missionary to instruct them, and they are not themselves able to fully understand the Gospel of God's Grace; alas! how truly sad and pitiable. Now all the church members implore the teachers of the Venerable Church

Assembly . . . to have compassion and send some lady missionaries to shepherd these women and girls; this is what the women
themselves earnestly hope for.[4]

Herbert had harassed the Zenana Mission, emphasizing the
Chinese reluctance to allow women to attend church, the
need for education for girls and Bible-reading classes for
Christian wives. He offered to buy a piece of land on which
to build accommodation for four women and a school with
'a splendid view of the [Xinzhou] plain and the mountain
ranges surrounding it',[5] taking money from his dental fund
to purchase the plot. His belligerent persistence obviously got
the better of the Zenana committee.

Herbert, aided by Chao, was quickly caught up with the
construction of new mission buildings. My great-grandparents had returned to Xinzhou with £1,000, collected through
gifts, the sale of embroidery, and a grant from the BMS. There
were plans to build homes for the missionaries and evangelists, along with a new hospital, boys' school and chapel. A
prominent site had been found close to the west gate, higher
on the hill and away from the 'fever hole'[6] of the mission's
present position on the small streets of the city. Herbert was
particularly taxed over the plans for the new chapel. What size
of congregation should he allow for? How great was his faith?
In the end, he decided on a hall suitable for their present
needs but one that could be extended to hold 500.

Herbert also maintained a demanding round of visiting,
preaching and medical work. A year's worth of dental patients
had missed his services and his shelves rapidly became a
'Museum of Casts'. He built an ice-house and in the winter

brought 20 tons of ice up from the river to preserve meat, provide cool drinking water and keep their butter from turning to oil in the summer. By way of relaxation he took up a battle with the Xinzhou district wolves, setting traps for them, and taking his gun out from time to time to hunt bustards, ducks, partridges, hares and rabbits for dinner.

Now free to engage more directly in ministry, Elizabeth accompanied Herbert on visits outside of Xinzhou, getting a good welcome from the women who gathered at the services. In the courtyard of their home she started a school with five girls, providing lessons in geography and reading, and teaching them to sing hymns. She did, however, employ a local schoolteacher because, as she told her aunt, 'teaching was never a hobby of mine'. The older local women vehemently opposed her plans.

'What good will that do them?'

'We have never heard of girls learning to read.'

We have managed without learning anything. Why can't they?'

The boys at the mission's schools, on the other hand, were enthralled with Elizabeth's initiative. It was a rule that the girls should not have bound feet and the boys were decidedly in favour of educated wives who had 'big feet'!

'They will be able to run about quickly like you, *Taitai*. And manage the house properly.'

This progress, however, came to a juddering halt in the autumn. Elizabeth suffered a stroke; her right side paralyzed. Sowerby was away, taking his wife and children to the coast on their return to Britain, and meeting the two new missionaries. The McCurrachs were in Taiyuan, struggling with the grief of losing their first child – sadly, their son had died two days after being born. Herbert was alone in caring for Elizabeth. He feared that her 'reason had gone' and attributed the stroke to her concern for the children. When several mailings arrived without letters from the boys, it had, he felt, 'brought on the crisis'. He was troubled that 'worry sometimes seems to be the breath of her life'. In a matter of a few days, the paralysis passed but Elizabeth's health was once again a major issue. When Sowerby returned with the new missionaries, Bessie Renaut and Sydney Ennals, a young minister from south London, Herbert himself broke down. He was 'fit for nothing either mentally or spiritually'. For a while, he could only find pleasure in his hunting escapades. It is perhaps as well that the winter weather brought the building programme to a seasonal halt.

As the nineteenth century came to its close, the tensions between the Chinese and the colonial powers that occupied her treaty ports, the foreign legations of Beijing, and numerous small Christian missions across north China began to surface, particularly in Shandong. In towns and villages across the province, a concoction of fear and fable was being mixed and used to poison relationships. In the countryside, resentment, turning to hatred, began to be focused on the missionaries and their converts. While Elizabeth and Herbert found time to recover from their ill health in Xinzhou, events elsewhere were beginning to unravel into violence. My great-grandmother was coming close to the end of her journey.

NOTES

[1] Charles T. Studd, 2 April 1893, quoted in N. Grubb, *C.T. Studd: Cricketer and Pioneer* (Guildford and London: Lutterworth, 1970), pp. 101,102. Used with permission: The Lutterworth Press.

[2] Adapted from T. Richard, *Forty-five Years in China* (New York: Frederick A. Stokes, 1916), p. 156.

[3] Quoted in letter from A. Sowerby to the BMS, 29 July 1899, quoted in 'Hsin Chow, Shansi, North China', *The Missionary Herald*, November 1899, p. 513.

[4] 'Appeal from North China', *The Zenana Missionary Herald* (part of *The Missionary Herald*), 1 July 1898, p. 363.

[5] 'In Loving Memory: Bessie Campbell Renaut', *The Zenana Missionary Herald* (part of *The Missionary Herald*), December 1900, p. 572.

[6] Letter from A. Sowerby to the BMS, Xinzhou, 29 July 1899, quoted in 'Hsin Chow, Shansi, North China', *The Missionary Herald*, November 1899, p. 513.

15

The Hour of Their Calamities

'Disturbances are to be feared from the foreign devils; every-where they are starting missions, erecting telegraphs, and build-ing railways. They do not believe in the sacred doctrines, and they speak evil of the gods . . . The will of heaven is that the telegraph wires be first cut, then the railways torn up, and then shall the foreign devils be decapitated. In that day shall the hour of their calamities come.'

Poster, Beijing, April 1900[1]

On New Year's Day, 1900, Elizabeth sat down to write to her brother, Ebenezer, and his wife, Nell. It is a short, chatty letter, full of incidentals about life in Xinzhou and flavoured with the essence of a good Christmas spent with her missionary colleagues. She had decorated the house with great boughs of white-berried mistletoe and placed pots of pungent yellow-centred narcissus in the living room. She had gone to great trouble to find the ingredients for plum puddings and had organized her five schoolgirls to make them for her guests at the Christmas dinner. Outside, heavy snow crusted the roofs and blanketed the streets but she, Herbert and Bessie were warm. Ten fires, fuelled by north China's rich coal seams, were being kept stoked by the servants day and night to keep the cold at bay. The warmth of the house and Elizabeth's contentment following a difficult autumn is written into the black ink, as clear on the onion-skin paper as the day she wrote it. The light touch of apricity in Elizabeth's letter would, doubtless, have been disturbed had she heard the news beginning to filter out of the district of Pingyin, 250 miles away in Shandong Province. The body of Reverend Sidney Brooks had been retrieved from a ditch. He had been decapitated.

Only 24, Brooks was a member of the Society for the Propagation of the Gospel in Foreign Parts (now the United Society for the Propagation of the Gospel). Having spent Christmas with his sister a day and a half's journey away, he was travelling by wheelbarrow through the snow to join another missionary in the county town. It was an anxious ride. There were bands of brigands attacking Chinese Christians north of the Yellow River, plundering and burning down properties, taking hostages and killing their victims. The only escape from these brazen daylight attacks was for the believers to renounce their faith. Twelve miles from sanctuary, Brooks was set upon by thirty armed men. They slashed at his arms and head with their swords, stripped away his outer garments and forced him to march for several hours before they stopped to eat. Brooks escaped and fled in the direction of Pingyin, but was no match for the three men on horseback who pursued him. His body was left where they hacked him to death.

This attack on Brooks was the first ripple of the violence that would soon convulse the foreign communities of north

China; the work of an enigmatic organization that had its impulse in a strange rebellion sweeping Shandong. In villages across the region, young men and women were flocking to see mass rituals in temples. Members of the *Yihetuan*, known as the Society of Righteous and Harmonious Fists, or the Boxers, were there to perform. They invoked the popular gods of Chinese culture, such as Sun Wukong, the monkey king, and Zhu Bajie, the pig, taking on animal characteristics in supernatural trances. The temple courtyards became arenas for fantastic pageants of martial arts; dozens of ecstatic young men spinning and dancing with swords. The performers shouted out to their audience. They were, they claimed, invulnerable to weapons and bullets, and challenged the watchers to come and attack them. There were female Boxers too – the Red Lanterns, whose name was derived from the lamps they carried to burn down buildings. They were said to have magical gifts of flight and the ability to pull down buildings with thin strands of cotton.

These spectacular shows of frenzied spirit possession were scripted with anti-foreign emotion. The Boxers played on natural resentment of colonial intrusion into Chinese territory and on the poverty and powerlessness of the common villagers who came to watch them. Foreigners brought goods and inventions that impoverished the Chinese. The *huoche*, 'fire carriages', that ran on iron roads benefited Herbert and Elizabeth and their colleagues, but to the locals they were a curse; they unsettled the graves of their ancestors. The mines that foreigners dug into Chinese wealth troubled the earth. The wind that groaned around rust-red telegraph wires transmitted the cries of the spirits. The church spires the missionaries erected disrupted the sensitive harmony of the laws of *feng shui*. The presence of the foreign devils was the reason for the floods and famines that beset the population. In 1898, the Yellow River had lived up to its reputation as 'China's Sorrow' and broken out from its shallow banks, swallowing up 2,500 square miles of countryside and 1,500 villages. The people were devastated and the Boxers gave them someone to blame.

For most rural Chinese, their only contact with foreigners were the missionaries, Protestant and Roman Catholic, who travelled further inland than merchants and government officials and who built houses and churches in their towns and villages. Foreign missionaries, however, were protected by their governments. It was, therefore, their converts who were the first targets for violence. The Boxers sent yellow cards to Chinese Christians inviting them to recant. To refuse was to run the risk of reprisal. Anti-Christian aggression was by no means a new phenomenon, but as New Year 1900 approached, this tide of resentment rose higher and higher until eventually, like the silted waters of the Yellow River, nothing could contain it. The killing of Brooks marked the breaking of a boundary into a new phase of the movement.

For Elizabeth, as she brought her cheerful letter to Ebenezer and Nell to a close, the news from Shandong was still a long way away.

Well, I must end this rambling Epistle. I am rather busy just now for our table boy was stupid enough to go and break his arm in a fight with the cook. I shall be glad to have a new photo of you all. We hope to soon send you one of our house and the farmyard which consists of three horses, cow, calf, big Mongolian dog, and a cart with two mules bringing wood and coal. Won't you come and spend your next holiday with us? We will give you a very warm welcome in more senses than one during the months of June, July and August.

Your affectionate sister,

Elizabeth.

After the difficulties of settling in, Elizabeth's stroke and the adjustments to be made with Bessie moving into their home, things were going well. There is renewed optimism in the letters my great-grandparents wrote to family and friends. They were having fun planting a row of seven poplars at the new mission site and setting out a line of small conifers to shield one of the garden walls. They were busy creating a well-stocked orchard – apple, apricot, peach, pear, plum and mulberry trees, plus four varieties of grapevine. My great-grandmother's health, although she suffered another bout of fever, improved as the winter gave way to spring. When Sowerby left to join his wife and family in Britain, Elizabeth was drafted into the hospital to help Herbert. She was delighted to receive her own gilded plaque from a father whose wife and baby she had nursed through a difficult pregnancy. The blue inscription was fixed over the main entrance, bearing testimony to the 'wonderful skill of the foreign lady and her foreign medicine'. The number of girls in her school increased to ten in spite of her insistence that they must have their feet unbound. She appointed a matron to help her; an intelligent seamstress who made Elizabeth and Herbert's clothes, and who quickly understood the *Jidu Jiao* ('Christ teaching') of her employer. One day, my great-grandmother found her weeping.

'I am a sinful old woman,' she told Elizabeth. 'All my life I have worshipped idols. Now I must go and empty my home of them.'

When the woman returned, she had her arms full of her gods, which she gave to Elizabeth.

'Do whatever you wish with them. I have no need of them.'

Later she allowed Elizabeth to cut open the bandages on her feet, a painful process, peeling back forty years of binding to reveal the broken arches and toes that she had squeezed into her tiny lotus shoes.

Both Herbert and Elizabeth continued to send letters to the children as frequently as the mail allowed, colouring their parental concerns over school reports, pocket money and winter clothes with tales of my great-grandfather's exploits with the wolves and their rides on their horses, Brownie, Daisy and Buttercup, into the countryside. Alongside encouraging Benjie to write to Mary as often as possible, reprimanding Charlie for taking up smoking, and asking Ridley to write more than his usual 'miserable little scraps', Elizabeth gleefully recounted their father's misadventures. 'I do enjoy a ride with father out to the villages,' she told my grandfather. 'One afternoon last week Daisy managed to stumble badly and I was so astonished to see father disappearing over the horse's head. Daisy bolted, if you please, while poor father was pulling himself together. Then Brownie wanted to go off full pelt after Daisy but I managed to keep him back and to stick in my saddle.'

There was a great deal for Herbert and Elizabeth to be thankful for, despite their obvious desire to be with the children. The work in Shanxi was bearing richer rewards in all areas of ministry: church planting, medical work and education. After sixteen years of struggle, the total number of church members had doubled in the last four years to over two hundred. In Xinzhou the new chapel was urgently required. At the Sunday services, Herbert preached with schoolboys packed in around his feet and the church doors were left open to allow an overflow into the courtyard. Chinese women believers now had their own service. The previous year's Chinese New Year conference in Taiyuan had also seen an increase in numbers. Four hundred believers had attended, some walking 130 miles, occasionally hitching lifts on coal carts and sleeping like tramps in makeshift kitchens along the route. Amidst fierce debates on foot binding and opium growing, there had been a moment of bemused controversy as the meetings drew to a close. At the final communion service Farthing requested that a Chinese brother 'give thanks for the cup'. A sturdy Mongol woman got to her feet. 'A good Christian woman – why not?' noted Farthing afterwards, adding for the benefit of sensitive readers of *The Missionary Herald*, 'Of course, it is not quite usual.'[2]

In his annual report, Sowerby summed up the situation in Xinzhou:

In every part of the work we can mark progress . . . With regard to schools, we have had a large accession of scholars this year, and the school is steadily developing into a high school for the most promising scholars . . . The number received by baptism is twenty-two [and] some eighteen converts from the northern out-stations are waiting over till next year . . . We have closed our mission year with a conference of our Christians . . . quite the best we have had. Never before have I been able to write a report with a heart so full of thankfulness and praise.[3]

The news of Brooks's death reached the mission at Xinzhou before the end of January. The discontent had spread west from Shandong into the neighbouring province of Hebei, where 'roughs and rowdies', as Herbert called them, were plundering the homes of Chinese Christians. Nevertheless, there was little anticipation that the violence would threaten the lives of the Shanxi missionaries. In their letters they seemingly had little fear for their own safety. Relationships with local people, which had been difficult in the past, had improved. The province's population was considered the 'most peaceable and law-abiding of the whole empire'.[4] Herbert and Elizabeth travelled to the villages without harassment, and reported to the British Foreign Office that they 'never had anything more unpleasant than an occasional difference with muleteers or innkeepers over payment'.

It was, perhaps, a naive optimism or an attempt to bolster confidence in the face of increasing difficulties. Elizabeth and Herbert must have watched the arrival of a new governor of the province in April with receding assurance of their safety; Governor Yuxian came with a troubled history. He had recently and rapidly risen to prominence as the governor of Shandong Province on the recommendation of a previous incumbent, Li Pengheng. Li had been dismissed for his handling of the murder of two German Roman Catholic missionaries. While the Chinese court publicly acceded to German demands for Li's dismissal, advising that he must not be 'mentioned for employment again', privately it manoeuvred him back into influence.[5] Yuxian followed Li's lead, encouraging the rise of the Boxers and leaving their rampages against Chinese Christians unchecked by his own troops. Yuxian was also demoted (a few days before Brooks was murdered) but, like Li, his public disgrace was a masquerade. In private he received the high honour of a scroll written by the Empress Dowager Cixi and in due time was restored to office in Taiyuan.

It is here that my experience in 2006 at the Summer Palace in Beijing and the lives of my great-grandparents touch. In simply seeing a large portrait of the woman they called 'Divine Mother' and 'Old Buddha' I found myself confronted with the knowledge that this woman and I were connected through them; though for Elizabeth and Herbert, the reality of that connection was far more brutal. The Empress Dowager sat at the apex of the Qing Dynasty. To those outside the walls of the Forbidden City, the inaccessible home of China's emperors, she was a chameleon in power; a woman about whom legends were more easily written than fact. A favoured concubine of the seventh Qing ruler of China, she imbibed the intrigues of court politics and fed off the power her position gained for her. As mother of the heir to the Dragon Throne, Cixi assumed supremacy as regent when the emperor died. From her reign 'behind the curtains', controlling first her son and then her nephew's monarchy, she played out her schemes like a marionette manipulator.

Cixi watched the Boxers with interest. Their sense of theatre attracted her and she was fascinated by their stories of possession by the gods. The Red Lanterns were intriguing; young women with powers that were considered equal to that of men. The Empress Dowager shared their loathing of the foreigners, who demanded more and more concessions from her country. She despised what she perceived to be the overly large feet, boat-like shoes, and hairy faces of Western women, whom she compared to cats, animals she could not abide. She abhorred Chinese Christians, whom she believed robbed their countrymen with lawsuits that missionaries supported, extracting money and property from neighbours for their own gain.

Ironically, six years earlier, the Chinese women of the Protestant churches of China had been busy gleaning money from all over the country on Cixi's behalf. A committee of missionaries in Shanghai was appointed to oversee the making of a special edition of the New Testament to present to her on her 60th birthday.[6] Each page was gilded with an ornate border and the book placed in a silver casket, etched with bamboo and birds and padded with gold plush, which was, in turn, encased in a teak box. The gift, 'The Sacred Classic for the Salvation of the World', was delivered to Cixi by the British and American Ambassadors, by 'a very happy coincidence . . . along with [the present] of Queen Victoria'.[7] Sadly, the Empress Dowager found no enlightenment in the gift, and her dim view of her Christian subjects did not change.

Cixi was intently aware of the political threat that an uncontrolled grass roots organization, like the Boxers, could pose to the weak Qing Dynasty, when there was so much unrest over corrupt officials and despair over lost crops. The argument in the echelons of power over whether to encourage or suppress the Boxers ebbed and flowed. When new posters started to appear declaring 'Support the Qing. Destroy the foreigners', the Empress Dowager found an ally. In time she would issue an edict declaring war on the colonial powers in China, and draw the Boxers into her armies. In the meantime, while she waited and watched, she dispatched Yuxian to take control of Shanxi.

In April, on the Sunday after Easter and three days after Yuxian's arrival, Elizabeth found space to write to Benjie, aged 14; this is her last surviving letter. She and Herbert were busy with a dispensary full of patients. My great-grandfather was 'constantly' away supervising the building of the new mission on the hill. She had been on a trek to one of the outstations to conduct a service, getting home in time for a meal and the evening English service that they held in their sitting room. She was happy to be well. They had planted out a garden and the fruit trees, which she hoped would grow 'into nice trees by the time you are ready to come and take up the work here. It is our constant prayer that we may live to see that day. . .' Whether the caveat that follows reveals her disquiet or is simply Victorian reticence, I do not know. In retrospect, it is a poignant, perhaps prophetic, addition: '. . . nevertheless not our will but his be done'. The letter closes with a line from a hymn:

'Tis to us no cause of sorrow, that we cannot tell to-day,
What it is will come to-morrow; 'tis enough that we can say:
'He whom we our Father call, knows the future – knows it all.'[8]

I am glad that Elizabeth, as she carefully folded this last letter to Benjie into its envelope, did not know the future.

NOTES

[1] Boxer placard, adapted from quote by S.B. Drake in 'Boxerism in Central Shantung', *The Missionary Herald*, December 1900, p. 549.

[2] G. Farthing, 'Mid-Shansi (North China) Christian Conference Annual Gathering', *The Missionary Herald*, August 1899, p. 389.

[3] A. Sowerby, 'Hsin Chow and the District', *The Missionary Herald*, May 1900, pp. 233,234.

[4] E.H. Edwards, *Fire and Sword in Shansi: The Story of the Martyrdom of Foreigners and Chinese Christians*, p. 42.

[5] Li Pengheng was instrumental in turning the Chinese court in favour of supporting the Boxers. Having failed to keep his promise that he would defeat the foreign forces and drive them out of China in the first battle, he committed suicide by poisoning himself in August 1900. His name has also been given as Li Pingheng.

[6] Cixi's date of birth was 29 November 1835, making her 59 years old in 1894 by Western counting. In China, traditionally, a newborn is one at birth and has their birthday at the Lunar New Year (January or February), rather than on the anniversary of their birth.

[7] Letter from M. Richard to A.H. Baynes, Shanghai, undated, quoted in 'Presentation to the Dowager Empress of China', *The Missionary Herald*, 1 March 1895, p. 94.

[8] T. Kelly (1769–1855), *Hymns not before Published* (Dublin: Thomas Johnston, 1815), p. 29. Elizabeth's letter reads: 'He whom we the [sic] Father call, "Knows the future, knows it all"'.

16

The First Death

'There is not much time. We are ready.'
                    Dr Arnold Lovitt, 28 June 1900[1]

As Yuxian settled into the governor's *yamen* at Taiyuan, posters
and pamphlets began to appear on the streets of the province's
main centres, inciting rumour and spreading the most bizarre
stories. Foreign ships had been seized off the coast and found
to have cargos of Chinese eyeballs, women's nipples and
vats of blood. In secret, the foreigners cut out paper men,
which came to life and wreaked havoc in the neighbourhood.
Beggars were being hired by malevolent Christians to poison
the nation's wells. Red marks that mysteriously appeared on
doorposts were the curse of the missionaries; the occupants
were certain to fall ill – some might die. Safety from these
evils could only be assured by passing on a Boxer pamphlet to
a neighbour. Ten copies would preserve a family; 100 copies
would be the salvation of a whole village.

Insidiously, suspicion and paranoia percolated into previously peaceful communities. It became difficult for strangers
to travel alone. Town elders posted guards over water sources,
and the city rich refused to drink water unless it had been

brought by their own servants from places they trusted. Water was wasted as villagers, believing that they were eradicating a threat to their lives, poured out buckets onto the ground. As in Shandong and then Hebei, it was only a matter of time before the situation in Shanxi reached its tipping point.

In mid-May, a mob gathered outside of the home of Elder Si, a Chinese Christian in a village 160 miles south of Xinzhou. The men attacked Si and broke into his home. Anything of value was plundered. Unwanted belongings were smashed or offered to the groups of onlookers. The mob moved on to the homes of other Christians. As they had done in the past, the Chinese believers appealed to the local magistrate. The magistrate arrested several of the Boxers and had one of them beheaded as an example to the others. The hostility died down. Yuxian, however, was not pleased with the magistrate's interference and had him dismissed. The news travelled north, unsettling the customary peace of the province. In Xinzhou these winds of unrest began to stir the population against Herbert, Elizabeth and their colleagues.

The first Boxers in Shanxi were the protégés of men that Yuxian is reputed to have brought from Shandong. Youths were attracted out of the villages of poor refugees, people who had abandoned their Shandong homes after the famines of the late 1870s and travelled west. In 1888, the failure of the spring rains in parts of north China again left the parched wheat crops dwarfed and thinly spread. That summer there were earthquakes. In mid-August furious rains swept away the harvests of millet and beans and the crops of tall sorghum. Cholera and starvation claimed victim after victim, leaving behind impoverished families whose fears could be manipulated by the Boxers. While Herbert was at home in Britain in 1898, drought stunted the autumn harvest around Xinzhou, reducing the wheat to dry, shrivelled sticks. It was the missionaries, the Boxers claimed, who brought famine on the people, standing through the night, naked, in the upper rooms of their houses, fanning away the clouds that carried much needed rain. Before long, local Shanxi peasants were also being drawn into Boxer ranks.

The last full letter I have from Herbert is dated 8 May 1900. Short of news, he entertained my grandfather with a horrific story of two Buddhist priests who had quarrelled over a nun. One, fearing for his life, had decided to blind the other. Having tipped scalding water over his rival's head and bound him hand and foot, the priest and an accomplice poked a wooden tobacco pipe stem into his eyes to remove them. When this cruelty failed in its malevolent objective, Herbert informed Benjie in roughly typed block capitals, 'the man actually seized them in his teeth and tore them out piecemeal.' It is perhaps fortunate that this was not the last communication Benjie ever received from his father! Elizabeth had dressed the blinded man's injuries and, while he would obviously never regain his sight, the wounds were healing rapidly. On a less dramatic and much happier note, Herbert had operated successfully on a man with cataracts – 'a blind man made to see'.

In retrospect, there was a splinter of disturbing news lodged in this letter, an indication of the growing resentment directed at the missionaries, though I doubt if Herbert or

Benjie recognized it at the time. My great-grandfather had been out to a village seventeen miles up the river valley. It had been a pleasant ride, the trees fresh with the greenery of spring, but:

> one thing made it very sad. One man brought in a little boy of six, who was desperately ill with pneumonia; he had brought him seven miles down a mountain pass on a donkey. I urged him to take the child back as soon as possible, but before he could start the child died. He had lost a little girl the week before, and he was beside himself with grief, and began to accuse me of having killed his children. I was so sorry for the poor fellow.

Beyond the middle of May there were no more regular letters from Herbert and Elizabeth to the children. It became impossible to get post out of the province to the coast. Official services were curtailed. Private couriers were stopped, their mail bags ripped open and the contents destroyed. When Herbert wrote to the bank in Tianjin requesting silver for their funds, he received no reply and no silver. Attempts to send telegrams were refused. Yuxian was slowly isolating the missionary community in Shanxi from the rest of China.

Elsewhere, events exploded into the first major incident of mass anti-foreign violence. In Hebei Province, railway lines were ripped up, a station set on fire, a bridge blown up and telegraph wires severed. At Baoding, a group of four foreigners were killed. Two missionaries, colleagues of Sidney Brooks, living fifty miles south of Beijing, were forced to abandon the safety of the magistrate's *yamen* by the back door and were chased through the streets of the city, before being captured and murdered by Boxers. In mid-June, a large force of Boxers stormed into Beijing, hacking down citizens connected with foreigners and attacking and torching foreign property. A week later, Cixi and her government ceased to equivocate. After an attack on Chinese fortresses close to Tianjin by colonial forces, they sided publicly with the Boxers and declared war: 'With tears have we announced war in the ancestral shrines . . . All our officials, high and low, are of one mind, and there have assembled, without official summons, several hundred thousand patriotic soldiers [the Boxers] . . . it will not be difficult to vindicate the dignity of our country.'[2] Officially, any foreigner in any part of China was now the enemy.

In Xinzhou, the situation deteriorated rapidly. As Herbert climbed the hill to supervise the work on the new mission premises, he passed Boxer houses with red cloths carrying the four-character phrase 'Preserve the dynasty. Destroy the foreigners' hanging out over the street. Placards were plastered up all over the city, blaming the Christian converts for the 'breach' with the people and warning them that 'Foreign religions are reckless and oppressive; disrespectful to the people and oppressive. The righteous people will burn and kill. Your judgements from heaven are about to come. Turn from the heterodox and revert to the true . . . If you do not repent there will be no opportunity for after-regret.'[3] And no one in authority was troubling to remove them. On 26 June, when an Imperial proclamation was posted throughout the province publicly supporting the Boxer cause, trouble broke out at nearly every mission station.

The previous day in Taiyuan, George Farthing had penned an anxious letter and given it to a courier to carry the forty miles north to Herbert. Spread over four sheets of paper it painted a bleak picture of the situation around the capital and Tianjin. Of great concern was an edict from the Empress Dowager instructing every governor and viceroy to 'have all foreigners residing within their borders wiped out'. Farthing found it hard to believe the report was true. Nevertheless, Governor Yuxian, he noted, was perfectly capable of carrying out such an order. 'I am deeply sorry to write you an alarmist letter,' he finished, 'my own wish is so to live as to be ready if the massacre should take place meanwhile going about as though I disbelieved it.'

Herbert sent a message back with a servant, but at sunrise the following day (29 June) the man returned. The letter was undelivered. Farthing's fears were being realized. There had been terrible trouble in Taiyuan. The gates of the city were all guarded and everyone wanting to enter was being searched. The servant had hidden the letter in a wall and gone into Taiyuan to find Farthing but the missionary's doors were barred and no one answered his calls. The news on the street was that the missionaries had fled and one of them, Edith Coombs, a Scottish teacher at the Schofield Memorial Hospital, was dead.

In the early evening of 27 June, a few boys had gathered at the narrow gate of the hospital and had thrown stones into the compound. It was a minor irritation. The staff went out to remonstrate with them. The youths sent them running back with another volley of rocks. A crowd started to congregate at the gate. Shouts of '*Sha*! Kill! *Shao*! Burn!' gathered momentum. A waiting room was set alight. The staff were no longer under any illusions. This was now a serious attack on their lives. Most of the Chinese servants and workers bundled out of the back door to escape into dark alleys, leaving behind eight missionaries, the toddler son of the hospital doctor, eleven Chinese schoolgirls and a handful of local staff. The group moved to one of the inner courtyards. For four hours they listened to the growing intensity of the attack while a mob surged into vacant rooms, pilfering whatever seemed of value and setting fire to the property. They retreated into a kitchen and then into a side room, until at midnight there was no further refuge and they were forced to flee.

Protecting the children as best they could, the men brandishing guns and a rifle, the group rushed out through the burning debris, across the courtyard and through the hospital gate. On the street, a huge bonfire barred their exit. They ran on through the gauntlet of fire and into the yelling crowd, taking blows on their arms and legs as they pushed their way down the road towards Farthing's house. When they finally arrived, there were only three of the schoolgirls with them. The rest had escaped or had been snatched away by the crowd to be sold into slavery.[4] Two of the Chinese women had been separated from the main group as they fled. Edith Coombs was missing.

In the morning, two Chinese friends of the mission went down to the hospital to view the damage. The street was strewn with debris, and the fire at the gate had died down to smouldering ashes. Amongst the embers lay Edith's charred skull and bones. She had made it beyond the gate but had gone back into the hospital grounds to help two of the girls who were struggling to escape. Both were new pupils to the school and had only recently had their feet unbound. Edith carried one out and returned for the second, a girl called Aitao. She tried to carry Aitao through the crowd but stumbled and fell. A man struck out at her with a stick. The mob surged forward and pelted Edith and Aitao with rocks. Prostrate and doing her best to shield the girl, Edith whispered into Aitao's ear, 'Don't be afraid, Aitao. We shall soon be where there is no pain or sorrow.'

But Aitao was pulled away and Edith was left alone to face her assailants. The men pushed the teacher into the flames. She tried to get away once, twice . . . and then could resist them no longer. She knelt in prayer. The crowd heaped burning sticks and wood onto her head and watched her burn to death.

Horrified by the servant's news, Herbert gathered his fellow missionaries around him – Elizabeth, Bessie Renaut, Sydney Ennals, Adam and Clara McCurrach, and Tom and Fanny Underwood, who were visiting Xinzhou from Taiyuan. He explained what had happened. There was a short, urgent discussion, and when it was finished they seemed to have little choice but to flee.

Everything was done hastily. Two carts were found. Three horses for the men. A mule litter for the women. Boxes were filled with clothing, bedding and food. Packing was harried and impromptu. Plans were hurriedly made and unmade, as each of them grabbed at things they may need. They must be away before the news from Taiyuan became widely known. A straggling train of animals and their luggage was assembled at the mission doors. Old He, Chao and a group of Chinese believers gathered, ready to leave with them. In the sultry dawn the makeshift procession climbed the hill towards the west gate and out onto the slopes above the river.

They headed south, briefly. Then west, travelling upstream along a river between banks of terraced hillsides. It was futile to seek help in Taiyuan, and there was news of danger in the north. Baoding, to the east, was clearly no longer safe and they would need to cross the Xinzhou plain, where they would be more easily spotted by pursuers. Here, at least, they were close to the comparative sanctuary of the yellow loess hills, a spread of low peaks threaded with ravines and winding paths.

At Xiahebei, one of the villages on the banks of the river, they found shelter in the home of a Chinese Christian, Chang. They had made little progress, just ten miles from Xinzhou, their company strung out along the uneven paths. Elizabeth was ill. They waited, sheltering in secret in Chang's courtyard, allowing the morning advantage to drift into the afternoon. At dusk an anxious messenger arrived. Soldiers were out hunting for them. They must move on.

The convoy reassembled and the courtyard gates were opened. They stepped out again onto the road. They had gone no further than a few hundred yards when Herbert stopped Chao. He must go to Shandong, to his home, if he could.

Chao protested, 'I will die with you.'

Herbert thrust money and a message into his hands and shook his head.

'No. If you can find help, then you may be able to save lives. We need you to go. There is nothing to be gained by the needless sacrifice of your life.'

Chao was still reluctant.

'There's one chance in a hundred we can escape. If not, we're not afraid. We will gladly lay down our lives for our Lord. If we die, others will come in our place. Go . . .'[5]

As Elizabeth and Ennals's cart passed, my great-grandmother leaned down.

'I have four children,' she told Chao. 'I can no longer give them a mother's care. But God can. Pray for them, Chao. Pray for them.'[6]

The last of the carts lumbered on, leaving Chao, their friend and co-worker of fourteen years, alone on the muddy pathway by the river.

NOTES

[1] Letter from Dr A.E. Lovitt to 'Friend', Taiyuan, 28 June 1900, quoted in E.H. Edwards, *Fire and Sword in Shansi: The Story of the Martyrdom of Foreigners and Chinese Christians*, p. 68.

[2] Proclamation dated 21 June 1900, quoted in M. Broomhall, ed., *Martyred Missionaries of the China Inland Mission* (London: Morgan and Scott, 1901), p. 303.

[3] Quoted in E.H. Edwards, *Fire and Sword in Shansi: The Story of the Martyrdom of Foreigners and Chinese Christians*, p. 58.

[4] All the girls were eventually located after the Boxer Rebellion and returned to their families or fostered by a Chinese Christian family.

[5] Chao Xiayun/H. Dixon, conversation adapted from letter from J.P. Bruce to the BMS, Chefoo, 10 November 1900, quoted in 'Our Martyred Missionaries', *The Missionary Herald*, January 1901, p. 7.

[6] E.M. Dixon, adapted from letter from J.P. Bruce to the BMS, Chefoo, 10 November 1900, quoted in 'Our Martyred Missionaries', *The Missionary Herald*, January 1901, p. 7.

17

Flight Across Shanxi

'We have often said we would rather walk with God in the dark
than alone in the light, and now we can prove to God our sincerity.'
Bessie Renaut, 18 July 1900[1]

It is difficult to know what delayed them so much as they left
Xinzhou, when they had, perhaps, their best opportunity to
put distance between themselves and the Boxers. After leaving
Chao, the company struggled on west along the river valley
for about an hour until it was clear that their luggage was
hampering progress. They turned off into a deep gully and
abandoned the carts, pushing their cases into a deep hole in
the sandy soil. More time was lost as the missionaries waited
in the dark for friends to bring donkeys. Perhaps Elizabeth's
poor state of health slowed them down. Ennals, too, seems to
have been unwell. Maybe they were simply caught between
hope and hopelessness. There were potential enemies in every
village. For better or for worse, they decided they must find a
hiding place, rather than run a gauntlet of uncertain hamlets
and unfriendly faces for days on end.

After midnight they stumbled on, following guides with
torches. Elizabeth and the two wives were on horses, Bessie

and Ennals on the donkeys, while the other men walked. They waded up a wide river bed and staggered over banks of deep sand, until their guides pushed on too far ahead and they were left without light. They were too frightened to call out, too petrified to stay where they were. In the darkness they lost the path and travelled a mile or more out of their way. Finally, they came to a narrow pass where they found their guides. The group scrambled up a rough track over the hills until, twenty-four hours after they had fled, they came to the village of Liujiashan, around fifteen miles south-west of Xinzhou. Daybreak forced them to retreat back into the hills. They could not risk being seen. It proved a miserable day. For nineteen hours the missionaries hid in a rocky glen, sitting out in heavy rain, while a torrent of water plunged down the hillside around their feet. It is no wonder that Elizabeth was ill.

Close to midnight, their Chinese companions arrived with lights and felt it was safe to guide them down into the village. Almost immediately, however, it was decided the men should move on; another march over the hillsides to hide in a cave. The four women were pushed down into a tiny cellar, an airless place, sealed by a lid. It 'almost cost them their lives', Herbert wrote in the diary he had begun to keep, 'they were pulled out only just in time'. A second cave was found for the women, and another day passed before the group could be reunited.

There are no descriptions of the caves in which the missionaries found shelter other than plain adjectives such as 'damp', 'dusty' or 'large'. These may, of course, have simply been holes excavated into the hillside, but they could have been homes or vacant store rooms. The hill people of Shanxi had dug themselves into the loess, constructing brick and stone house fronts to caverns, complete with doors and windows. On hillsides these houses were stacked up, terrace upon terrace, connected by narrow footpaths which hurried from door to door.

Herbert, Elizabeth and their colleagues settled to an uneasy existence. For ten days they lived in the home of a Chinese believer. His hollowed-out house stood at the head of a narrow gully with steeply sloped hills on either side, an isolated position which could be more easily defended if they were attacked. Propriety was, nonetheless, maintained; some of the men slept in a straw hut. To pass the time, Herbert, Bessie and Ennals jotted notes into diaries and Adam McCurrach wrote letters home. These they intended to give to their Chinese friends to smuggle down to the coast or, failing that, they planned to bury them in the walls and floor of caves, hoping that other missionaries would find them. They were entirely dependent on the Chinese believers who, at risk to their own safety, visited sporadically, bringing much-needed food supplies and snippets of news.

There was rarely good news. Across the province there were stories of churches and Christians under attack from the Boxers. On Saturday, as the missionaries had sheltered in the glen, Elizabeth's cook and servant had appeared, having walked through the rain to find them. Herbert immediately dispatched them to Taiyuan to find out what was happening. In the early evening, three days later, they returned clutching a slither of paper on which Farthing had scribbled a brief message: 'We are here marked out by the Governor for death and only God has caused it to be so long delayed. He will work for our deliverance. Just now we are prisoners – the first that will fall if the blow should come.'

Herbert sent the cook off again, with a note hidden in his hat string, heading for Baoding or Beijing or Tianjin, or wherever he could find foreign troops and help.

The missionaries seemed caught in limbo. A becalmed place between the desire that one of their messages would bring salvation, and the knowledge that there was the imminent possibility of death. In a letter to his mother, McCurrach wrote: 'We are now in very great danger of losing our lives . . . there is absolutely no means of escape. It is very dark. I can't say more. Clara and I have been praying for you one by one. If we die, I trust it is together, and then we shall enter heaven together and together receive our crowns.'[2]

The following day, Ennals wrote in his diary: 'I do not regret I came to China, and although my life will have been short, it will in some way have fulfilled the Master's will. I pray earnestly for his deliverance and feel we shall have it . . . These days of quiet have helped us to see the Saviour's face.'[3]

The history of nineteenth-century mission is in many ways a catalogue of men and women who died taking their faith to another nation, through natural disasters, sickness or violence. It is perhaps easy for some to dismiss these attempts to express their feelings as pious. I can only imagine what it felt like to sit on that hillside day after day, straining to hear a hostile footfall against a stone on the path, the discordant murmur of unfamiliar voices, or trying to write a few meaningful letters to people I loved and never expected to see again.

Of the group, Ennals was perhaps the least fortunate. Shanxi Province had not been his original designation. He had been assigned to work in Shandong, but had made an arrangement with a co-worker to swap stations.

With the last of his ink running out, Herbert wrote to his children:

My dear Bennie, Charlie, Mary & Ridley
Mother and I are in great danger of being killed by the Governor of the province but God has led us hitherto. We have had to hide in gullies and caves in the mountains away to the west of Xinzhou . . . If we live you shall hear all about it: if we die we shall meet later in heaven.
Your affectionate Father
Herbert Dixon.

On the following Sunday (8 July), perhaps heartened by the passage of time without detection, they held an open-air service. Monday and Tuesday passed quietly. But on Wednesday there was a commotion in the village. Men had carried one of the villagers back over the hills from his daughter's home, five miles away. He had been beaten badly by Boxers for supposedly poisoning wells for foreigners.

'The Boxers intend to mount a raid in two days' time,' he told them.

Late that evening, a messenger arrived.

'The people of Xinzhou have rioted. They are angry that the officials allowed you to escape. A hundred Boxers have set out to destroy the homes of the Roman Catholics. They will come here to kill you.'

Herbert grabbed a few moments to record the details in his diary. They must walk through the night, further into the hills, to a new dig that their friends had been working on. They advised the Christian villagers to flee for their own safety, and then packed up as many of their own belongings as they could carry.

There is no record of which Chinese friends went with them on this journey. From Herbert's diary it appears that only Old He remained with them, but there may have been one or two others. The new 'cave' was no more than a damp hole in the loess bank, just large enough to lie down in. They carried rough oatmeal bread, some biscuits, tins of sardines and milk with them, but with no one to supply more food, these were strictly rationed. Water could be collected from a stream but they possessed only two buckets and the stream was a mile away. Their bedding was wet and it was impossible to dry it for fear it would be seen from the tops of neighbouring hills. At night they slept outdoors. During the day they had no choice but to hide in the cave, waiting in silence.

It was here that they received the news that they dreaded. The missionaries at Taiyuan were dead. All of them. The men, the women and all eight of the children. Herbert called Old He and gave him a message to take to Baoding, once again requesting help. Tragically, the evangelist never made it beyond Xinzhou. On the way, he stopped at his sister's home and was spotted by youths, who carted him off to the magistrate. When asked to reveal the missionaries' whereabouts he refused. The magistrate ordered him to be thrashed with bamboo rods. He was beaten until he was almost insensible, thrown into prison and locked in the stocks. For three days he was tended to by a Christian imprisoned with him, but he was barely able to drink and on the fourth day he died. He had taken more than a few blows for Jesus. He was Xinzhou's first convert and probably its first martyr.

Old He was not the only one of my great-grandparents' friends to be killed. Chang, the owner of the home at Xiahebei in which they first sheltered, was caught on his way to visit the missionaries by people who resented him not paying temple taxes. Like Old He, he refused to show the Boxers where the foreigners were hiding, and was beaten to death with their sticks and swords. Ennals recorded the plight of members of their Chinese congregations in other towns: 'There has been trouble at each of our north stations . . . [at] Fanshi two Christians are burnt, one being the evangelist. At Daizhou the mission place is burnt. At Guoxian the mission place has been looted. At Qicun the mission place has been looted. At Gaocheng one Christian, taken by his heels and dragged around, was killed. Truly the persecution is dreadful.'[4]

Not all the Chinese believers were courageous. The authorities made wooden tablets to be hung outside houses with the inscription 'I belonged to the foreign church, but now I have left it, and hereafter I will follow the customs of China'.[5] There are no records of the names of those who received them or whose relatives and neighbours, in a desperate attempt to save them, went to the authorities on their behalf. The Shanxi church, however, did not condemn them, and when the troubles were over, those prepared to burn the tablets and repent were accepted back into membership.

On Monday, 16 July Herbert seems to have been at his lowest point since fleeing Xinzhou. Writing now with a pencil, he noted: 'Heavy rain all morning – mountains enveloped in mist. No one has been near – How long can we hold out? Only few biscuits, sardines & milk – Sad to see wasting of the ladies' faces – Mrs. D almost gone this morning . . . our position grows more and more desperate humanly speaking. But God is our Refuge & Strength.' Then he recorded the amounts owed to the mission and himself by the outstations; putting his affairs in order, perhaps in the knowledge that hope of rescue was fading fast.

There are only a few more entries in his diary.

Tuesday 17 July – Last night God sent us more food & a man to carry us some water . . . they say some of the villagers are plotting to betray us, or to prevent food reaching us to starve us to death. Rumours come this afternoon of Boxers coming up from Taiyuan to hunt us to death. We are still in God's hands.

Wednesday July 18 – Last night heard firing in village just below us. This morning at 6.15 a.m. a man came to our cave and said he himself had seen 30 or 40 Boxers. He offered to lead us to a cave about a mile away. We prayed for guidance and decided to abandon all the bedding we could not carry, to bury all milk we could not carry and after a hurried march exposed to view on the mountain side we have arrived at said cave.

God knows all about it, and we trust him to save us – but are willing to die if that be God's will.

Thursday July 19 – four people from two villages brought us some coarse food in exchange for silver – but supply very scanty & unpalatable . . . all roads blocked against any supplies being bought for us. Local supplies are exhausted but God has supplied us day by day with something. We have no other news and know not how long we can go on. Mrs. D ill again today.

Saturday July 21 – About 11 last night a man came with some boiled millet. He said that he had seen three Boxers from Tai Yuan drilling the people: all bent on finding and attacking us. As we do not mean to fight we can only run for our lives, and so had once more to pack up and march by night back to our first cave on the other side of the watershed. On the march Mrs. D fell three or four times from utter exhaustion and had finally to be carried in unconscious.

Herbert's frustration and anger pour out onto the last pages of his diary:

The utter uncertainty of our position, and lack of all news from the outside makes us dependant on mere local rumours brought to us by an opium smoker as the Christians have all had to run for their lives. Were it not for trust in God we should be in utter despair. To see the ladies, and especially my dear wife in her weakness, have to tramp over these rough mountains by night, and be hiding all day on wet bedding in damp or dusty caves without proper food and without water to wash themselves, makes me think some very bitter thoughts against the Governor of the province who has promoted this terrible persecution . . . O Lord, relief come soon! Chao gone east 22 days. Cook gone east 17 days. He gone east 10 days and Wen gone north 8 days. God grant some of them may have got through . . . Our love to our children & all friends.

An hour and a half after my great-grandfather wrote these words, Boxers appeared on the mountain above their cave. They were ready to attack.

NOTES

[1] B.C. Renaut, 18 July 1900, diary entry quoted in R.C. Forsyth, *The China Martyrs of 1900*, p. 63.

[2] 'Adapted from letter from W.A. McCurrach to his mother, Shanxi, 3 July 1900, quoted in R.C. Forsyth, *The China Martyrs of 1900*, p. 58.

[3] S.W. Ennals, adapted from diary entries 4 and 8 July 1900, quoted in R.C. Forsyth, *The China Martyrs of 1900*, pp. 60,62.

[4] S.W. Ennals, adapted from diary entry 6 July 1900, quoted in R.C. Forsyth, *The China Martyrs of 1900*, pp. 60,61. I have not been able to identify all the modern names of the places listed in Ennals's diary entry. The names given are derived from Ennals's original spellings and their probable locations are as follows: Fanshi – Fan Shih; probable location Fanshi, approx. sixty miles north-east of Xinzhou; Daizhou – Tai-chou; probable location Daixian, approx. forty-five miles north-east of Xinzhou; Guoxian – Kuo Hsien; probable location Guoyangzhen, approx. thirty miles north of Xinzhou; Qicun – Chi Ts'un; probable location Qicun, approx. ten miles north-west of Xinzhou; Gaocheng – Chao Mon Chong; possible location Gaocheng or Caozhang, approx. ten miles north/north-east of Xinzhou.

[5] W.Y. Fullerton, 'Our China Tour: Hsin Chow and Shou Yang', *The Missionary Herald*, November 1908, p. 336.

18

A Final Journey

'To live in hearts we leave behind is not to die.'

Thomas Campbell, 1825[1]

About 9 a.m. heard shouting of 'Pastor', 'Pastor' – then silence
. . . then saw one, two, three, four men, on top of mountain
evidently watching our cave mouth. This went on till about 2.45
p.m. when suddenly an attack was commenced by men above
the cave hurling immense stones at the small mouth of the cave.
Fearing we should be blocked in, McCurrach and I dashed
out and amid a hail of huge stones commenced firing with a
revolver and a gun at the more prominent leaders. One man
with a yellow cap was most persistent, so I gave him a charge of
N° 1 shot . . . the wounded man rolling over & over down the
hillside into the gully below us. They began to run up the hill.
Then gradually the crowd of fifty or sixty streamed away over the
ridge down to a village below and left us the field.

Above the cave where they had first gathered, we found one
of our Xinzhou church members with a terrible gash in his head
and his throat cut. It was evident he had been dead some hours,
and as his hands were bound behind him with a leading rope,
it was evident they had caught him on the mountains and had

led him captive to see the attack. The dear fellow had shouted to
warn us and had been killed on the spot.

They killed him simply because he was Christian.

These are the last words written by Herbert that I have. The
pencil fades from the page. That evening he, Elizabeth, the
McCurrachs, the Underwoods, Sydney Ennals and Bessie
Renaut sat out on the hillside in the warmth of a summer's
evening. It was a relief to come out of hiding in their cramped
cave and enjoy the beauty of the Shanxi mountains. At their
side lay the wounded Boxer, groaning over his injuries. He
was aged around 20, the captain of 100 men, sent by the
Xinzhou magistrate, he said. The Boxers had abandoned him
in the gully but Herbert's bullet had done no serious damage.
Herbert cleaned the wound, a graze to the head, and they
carried him up to the cave where he would be safe from the
wolves that prowled the night. All around them were the
sharp-edged boulders that had been thrown down over the
entrance and which could have sealed them into a living
tomb. It was, as Bessie wrote in her final entry to her diary, as
though 'the beauty of [the scenery] seems mockery'.[2]

Their thoughts turned to Psalm 70:

Make haste, O God, to deliver me; make haste to help me, O
LORD.
Let them be ashamed and confounded that seek after my soul:
let them be turned backward, and put to confusion, that desire
my hurt . . .
O God: thou art my help and my deliverer; O LORD, make no
tarrying.[3]

There was brave talk of hope of a rescue, but they must have known that the likelihood of foreign troops arriving was remote. Their remaining friends had fled. There would be no more news of the outside world: of what was happening in Beijing, Baoding, Tianjin, Taiyuan or even Xinzhou. Food supplies were low and would not be replenished. The Boxers knew where they were. It may be a day or two before they summoned up the courage to attack again, but there seemed little doubt that they would return. Travelling on was out of the question. Even if the others could summon the strength to climb the hills once more, Elizabeth was in no condition to walk much further. They could only bury their last letters and diaries in the walls and floor of the cave, hiding away the final words they wanted their families and friends to remember them by, and wait for the Boxers to make their next move.

All that remained of the lives of my great-grandparents was told afterwards when the BMS missionaries returned to Shanxi and pieced together these last shreds of story which were passed onto them. There were no more attacks from the Boxers. Instead, four days later, on 25 July, a troop of Imperial soldiers arrived from Xinzhou. The missionaries did not capitulate lightly, but resistance was futile and, after repulsing an attempt to capture them, they surrendered and allowed themselves to be escorted back to the city.

There is no record of the reception they received as they re-entered Xinzhou; a bedraggled procession of convicts in the custody of soldiers. The eight missionaries must have presented a woeful appearance in their tattered Chinese clothing, soiled by long hours lying in caves, their faces thinned by exhaustion and lack of food, their crumpled bodies portraying the bleakness of their four-week ordeal. It is unlikely that they saw much sympathy in the gazes of their former neighbours. Two of the mission houses were broken down to uninhabitable ruins and two others so gutted that only their roofs, scorched with the black of burning, remained. Their guard took them to the *yamen*, where their interview with the hostile magistrate was simply a preliminary to imprisonment.

A 'tiger's mouth', the name the Chinese gave to a prison, was a foul place for a prisoner. There was nothing of comfort and everything to demean the inmates, squatting or lying in filth for endless hours. At the height of the Shanxi summer the temperature escalated to over 30 degrees centigrade. The humidity saturated them in rolling sweat and sapped what little strength they had left. It is difficult to imagine the fetid smells that assaulted them, or the crawling discomfort that the lack of personal hygiene would breed. If rats had been a problem in the city, here they must have been a plague. One day lingered into three. Then a week. And on into a second week.

Their plight remained unresolved until 8 August, when officials brought the first piece of good news they had received in over a month. A deputy official with ten soldiers had arrived from Taiyuan. There were new orders from the governor, Yuxian. They were to be escorted out of the province to the safety of the coast. They would leave the following day.

It was just before dawn on Thursday, 9 August, that four wooden carts trundled into the courtyard of the city prison.

Ragged and weak, Elizabeth emerged wearily into the slender daylight. My great-grandfather, his beard matted, his clothes stained, stood with her, the others grouped around them. There was a reassuring normality to the preparations. Four carts for eight people, as would be expected. There was food piled up for the journey. The missionaries made themselves as comfortable as they could manage. Their long trek to the coast commenced. There were no last-minute orders to return them to their cells. No one called them back as they turned out into the streets.

The carts took them down the hill towards the dusty brown tiers of the pagoda above the east gate, beyond which lay the road out across the plain and the route towards Baoding and Tianjin. The vehicles were manoeuvred through the archway of the inner gate and into a darkened hallway of stone, a corridor a few yards wide trapped between high walls. The procession came to a halt. They must wait until the outer doors were opened.

They sat in the deep well of the gateway, while above them the night sky yielded to shades of blue, and up on the parapets the yellow flames of crude torches paled against the dawn. Behind them the gates scraped shut. But the outer gates remained bolted. There were men on the walls. And into the stillness fell the cold cry of command.

'*Sha*! Kill!'

It must be horribly degrading to be forced to strip naked before a mob of men. To experience the utter humiliation of removing article after article of clothing until nothing is concealed. This was far beyond the 'usual' stripping to the waist demanded at public executions. It is difficult to imagine the horror that my great-grandmother, used to modest clothing covering from ankle to shoulder, would have felt as she fumbled over Chinese buttons and pulled away the intimacies of British lacing. And then to know that your journey is over and the swing of a soldier's sharpened blade will sever your union with life, your dear children and the people you have given all for . . .

As the sword blows fell on my great-grandmother's head, shoulders and neck, Herbert rushed across to her. The swipe of a sword felled him. He dropped, senseless, into the dirt. There was no escape. There was no stay in the onslaught. Within a few minutes, Elizabeth left the air as quiet as the dawn.

It was a sordid affair. The gates of the city were opened and the corpses tossed down by the river, where they lay exposed to be demeaned by passers-by and rooted at by animals, until a non-Christian friend of Herbert's hired beggars to gather up their remains in mats. He had the bodies buried, the men on one side, the women on the other, in the shadow of the Xinzhou walls and beneath the sparse shade of birch trees, while he burned incense and read a funeral address he had composed.

I do not know how my great-grandparents made that final parting, but it is clear they were secure in their faith and the promise of life to come. Herbert had told Chao, as they said their goodbyes on the first evening of their flight from Xinzhou, that he was not afraid to die. He would, I know, have found courage in the glory of martyrdom that imbued Victorian Christian mission.

The final agony for Elizabeth was raw. A very sick woman, bereft of Herbert's support during her last moments, her heart gripped by grief for her soon-to-be-orphaned children far away in Britain. This was evil – a visible, tangible and vile evil – but it would not achieve its desired goal to rid China of Christians. I am sure my great-grandmother prayed, but I will never know if she repeated Jesus' words from his cross, 'Father, forgive them; for they know not what they do.'[4] Forgiveness was to come. But from another quarter and in another century, close to this spot, where she fell and where she died.

NOTES

[1] T. Campbell, 'Hallowed Ground'. First published as 'Stanzas', *New Monthly Magazine*, Vol. 14, September 1825, p. 289.
[2] B.C. Renaut, diary entry 21 July 1900, quoted in R.C. Forsyth, *The China Martyrs of 1900*, p. 63.
[3] Psalm 70:1,2,5b (KJV).
[4] Luke 23:34 (KJV).

Xinzhou
17 October 2006

19

An Unexpected Trip

'The meaning is in the waiting.'

R.S. Thomas, 1968[1]

The October sun was shining – at least it was trying to – through the polluted air. Crackling underfoot from the dead maize lying on the dry, rocky ground and the cries of squawking crows above were the only sounds that disturbed Stuart, my husband, Christine, our friend, and I as we walked across a field on the rise above Xinzhou city. We were a sombre little group – three English, six local Chinese Christians, and our driver, Zhang – watched by some bemused locals from their dilapidated donkey cart. In the centre of the field lay the scattered, shattered stones of a large memorial. Below us was the city where Elizabeth and Herbert had lived and died, and where my grandfather had spent his early years. Now here I was, standing in front of the ruins of a monument to the martyred missionaries.[2] Carved into one of the great granite blocks I could trace with my fingers the names of my great-grandparents alongside those of their colleagues. Lying nearby was another flat stone commemorating forty Chinese Christians who had also died in that fateful summer of 1900.

My emotions were already fragile. Things were happening so fast; too fast. The past and the present were meeting. I was at the heart of God's plans in a way I had never expected. We stood. We looked. We asked questions. Seeing the broken stones lying around on the rough ground made these moments all the more poignant. This was proof, as if we needed it, that it was here that Herbert and Elizabeth had fulfilled their undertaking to tell others the truths of their Christian faith.

Afterwards, our Chinese hosts took us down the hill into the city. We stopped at the east gate, a new structure being rebuilt as a replica of the original gateway, the entrance and exit enclosing an inner courtyard. This was where the massacre happened. Where eight lives were ended. Where the lives of others changed forever. Where family histories were rewritten. The reality of the brutal killings overwhelmed me. It was heartbreaking that the violent hatred of men had caused such carnage. I spoke into my mini tape-recorder describing the scene, my voice breaking as I relived the event in my imagination: 'I feel dreadful as I stand here and think how brave they were. They were expecting to be let out. They were expecting to go back to England and see their children. Instead, they were hauled down from the cart and beaten to death.'

My grief surfaced uncontrollably as I spoke. So long ago, yet so close. Their faith, my faith. Their God, my God. In my confused, emotional state, my tears flowed and the recording captured my pain.

I have only one childhood recollection that links me to China. It is a scene etched into my memory. I am 6, maybe 7, years old, wearing a rather tight, over-washed T-shirt and shorts, my chubby arms and legs brown from a summer holiday spent with my grandparents in south Devon. I am standing alongside my grandfather, now retired from his medical practice in Bristol. We are in his garage, which smells of paint, oil and wood shavings. He is working at his bench, pouring green resin into a red plastic mould; the mould of a miniature Chinese figure. I watch him intently. I have no memory of having much of a conversation. I just wondered why he was making these little models, and felt uneasy.

I don't remember my grandfather ever talking about China, or his parents. Around his house there were a few bronze Chinese urns, small links to his childhood. Nor do I have any recollection of my grandfather speaking about the effect the death of his parents had on him as a youth of 14. I am sure that the hurt was very deep and stayed with him throughout the rest of his life. Suddenly and unexpectedly everything changed completely. Now, he was head of the family.

Early in November 1900, Benjie, Charlie, Mary and Ridley received the definite confirmation of their parents' horrendous deaths. It wasn't until 13 December, however, that a memorial service was arranged at Bloomsbury Chapel in central London for the Xinzhou martyrs. In my family's black box I found a copy of the service sheet. Written at the bottom of the page is a note in my grandfather's hand, 'Charlie and I went to this service and saw Mr Baynes [the BMS Secretary] afterwards. It was a touching meeting, the place was crowded.' No doubt it was crowded, with stunned family and friends sitting alongside two young boys grappling with what had happened to their parents; two teenagers becoming men as the reality of their loss hit home. I can only reflect on what it was like to listen to Sowerby and others trying to explain what had happened; making clear that God was and still is in control of life; speaking to them of the Christian's secure hope of life after death; finishing with the challenge to follow in the footsteps of these martyrs. In letters to Timothy Richard and the BMS, my grandfather wrote of returning to China as a medical missionary but, for reasons I do not know, it was never to happen.

Nearly a year after Elizabeth and Herbert died, a very different memorial service took place in Xinzhou. The political situation had changed. The Boxer Rebellion was long since over. Just five days after my great-grandparents' deaths, troops of the foreign powers had seized control of Beijing. Cixi had fled to Xian. Now a treaty was being formulated to appease her adversaries. On 29 July 1901, a group of the local gentry and officials in dark robes and conical hats gathered in the *yamen* with three members of a 'Missionary and Peace Commission' for the formality of tea and a round of grand introductions before the company set out in procession for the east gate. There were banners and musicians and wreaths of flowers and great rolls of satin, which were inscribed with the names of the martyrs, suspended on bamboo poles carried by two men. An account written at the time captures the emotions of that day:

On the very spot where our dear friends were killed a coloured cloth awning with a platform for a table etc. was erected. The place is between the inner and outer gates of the city wall, very narrow and confined. Here the service was held, attended by the officials and Christians, and as many more as could get access or see from the wall. The address, scripture, and prayer were read by Chao. The memories and the occasion were far too strong to allow for extempore speech.

The cortège walked on to a small graveyard on high ground amongst corn and millet fields outside the city wall. The site looked out over the southern expanse of the Xinzhou plains to mountains in the east, where the missionaries had sometimes retreated during the hot summer months.

First went the officials in their chairs, next the gentry, then came the musicians and foot-soldiers, next the cavalry, then another band, then the Christians, and then the missionaries in their chairs. Then followed the scrolls and wreaths carried in small pavilions. The rear was closed by another company of cavalry. We wound through the thronged streets, out by the south gate and suburb, and then turned west to the hill where the cemetery is.[3]

The cemetery was enclosed within a walled garden of trees, and decorated with flowers in large plant pots. Eight graves lay in a neat line, each plot eventually to be marked with a tall, stone cross bearing the missionary's name. At the centre rested the graves of Elizabeth and Herbert, flanked by those of the other women on the left and those of the men on the right.

There we found a great crowd assembled . . . The banners and wreaths were first arranged by the side of the tent covering the graves. Then, when we had all assembled in this tent, with the officials ranged on one side and we and the Chinese Christians on the other, a specially appointed Mandarin read an address. After this we had a short Christian service, to which all the officials courteously remained. Thus the sad memorial service was over.[4]

All of this happened over a century ago, and yet the memory of the martyred missionaries lives on in Xinzhou. While sepia photographs remain, the graves are gone and the memorial erected by the BMS in 1910 lies broken in a field of maize. But the contribution of my great-grandparents and their colleagues to the Christian faith in Shanxi Province can still be seen in the local believers, who know each martyr's name. It is a powerful testimony that these lives, given in the service of Jesus Christ, have had an effect for good over one hundred years later.

There were times when our arrangements for travelling in China didn't seem to be going to plan. We wondered what on earth God was doing when what seemed like a well-organized itinerary started to fall apart. With a large calendar laid out on the floor of our living room, Stuart and I planned and re-planned, crossing out dates and destinations as often as we wrote them in. Our initial thought was to take our trip from June to September. In the end, we decided to travel from September to December.

Actually, we were surprised to be in north China at all. It was not somewhere we had ever dreamed of going. As our plans for our sabbatical were discussed, China squeezed itself very neatly between stops already scheduled in Nepal and New Zealand. We could visit friends working in Shanghai, Xian and Chengdu.

'Why not try to visit the place where your great-grandparents worked?' was the prophetic suggestion made by our churchwarden.

Right up to the last moment, our plans kept being adjusted. Belatedly, we discovered that China had a week-long public holiday at the beginning of October when any travel would be very difficult for foreigners, and even as we travelled alterations occurred. Little did we know that God was behind every change.

We arrived in Beijing on 7 October and flew to Taiyuan where we were helped by Andrew Kaiser, a young American. Meeting him was another of God's provisions for us as my knowledge of the Boxer Rebellion was sketchy to say the least. Andrew had made a detailed study of the Christian history of Shanxi Province. He took us to visit some of the sites where Herbert and Elizabeth worked when they first arrived in China. The old missionary hospital, built of brick and grey stone, was still there; a long, two-storey Victorian building with deep sash windows. We saw the site where the Taiyuan missionaries were killed. These were my great-grandparents' friends. Later, on my return home, I found copies of letters they had written to each other with their warnings about the Boxers. After two days in the city, my mind was spinning. I felt emotionally drained from engaging with the horrors of the Taiyuan massacre. We changed our plans once more. The visit to Xinzhou must wait. We needed a rest day.

We chose to spend a day at Pingyao, a Ming Dynasty walled city that is now a UNESCO World Heritage site, fifty miles south of Taiyuan. It is like a nineteenth-century town, and gave me a feel of how life must have been for Elizabeth and Herbert in Xinzhou. As I wandered around the roads, I could picture my great-grandparents walking down similar streets, passing shops resembling those I saw, speaking with people like those I met. We watched the inhabitants going about their daily business with few concessions to modern life; no cars are allowed, only bicycles, or carts drawn by donkey or bullock. Food was being cooked on street corners and there were eating houses where soups, noodles and tea were served. We visited small shops where young girls were making slippers by hand, and admired the city's classical architecture. Surprisingly, we encountered no other Europeans, but there were plenty of Chinese tourists.

Next morning, Stuart, Christine and I, with our luggage, squeezed back into Zhang's Ford Fiesta and headed for Xinzhou. We had no idea what we would find. Would any memory of my great-grandparents still remain? What was the state of the Xinzhou church? All we had was a phone number for the current pastor. The day that followed was full of those 'God moments' that write deep into the memory the biblical truth of God's sovereignty and his willingness to answer his children's most outrageous prayers. Our arrival on that particular Tuesday morning at that particular time had a divine hand behind it. God's timing was to prove impeccable.

We arrived in Xinzhou, and Zhang phoned the pastor.

'*Bu zai.*' He was out. Not an encouraging start!

The pastor's wife gave Zhang instructions. We turned off the main road and negotiated our way down nondescript streets flanked by large blocks of grey concrete apartments. There were few pedestrians out on the streets, and those that were stared at us in surprise. Zhang pulled up beside a small group of five people waiting on the pavement; the pastor's wife had informed them of our imminent arrival. They led us into one of the high-rise buildings and to a small grey room furnished with only an old wooden table and plastic chairs. A little white dog occupied a small mat on the concrete floor.

The three women and two men appeared very serious. It was clear as they formally welcomed us that they were a little suspicious of who we were and why we had come. But when Zhang explained who I was – the great-granddaughter of Herbert and Elizabeth Dixon – the room erupted into smiles, handshakes and hugs. I didn't know these people but suddenly, now my identity had been revealed, they seemed to know me. I was astounded by their delight. It was as if they had been expecting me. And in some way they had. This group of Xinzhou Christians had been praying for three months for a relative of one of the martyred missionaries to make contact with them. They had no other option but to pray, trusting that God would hear them, and he did. What a prayer of faith! To many this would seem an impossible request, but God is a God of the impossible. Here I was, in this unpretentious apartment in a mundane backstreet of an ordinary Chinese city, the answer to their prayers. It didn't fully dawn on me until later that we were only there on this day because they had prayed and God had intervened in our plans. The meaning had been in the waiting.

NOTES

[1] R.S. Thomas, 'Kneeling', *Not That He Brought Flowers* (London: Hart-Davis, 1968), p. 32. Used with permission: Kunjana Thomas.

[2] I do not know when the monument was so badly damaged. It is possible that this occurred during the Cultural Revolution when so much of China's heritage was destroyed.

[3] Adapted from M.B. Duncan, 'Public Funeral in Honour of Our Martyred Missionaries in Hsin Chou, Shansi Province', *The Missionary Herald*, November 1901, pp. 509,510.

[4] Adapted from E.H. Edwards, *Fire and Sword in Shansi: The Story of the Martyrdom of Foreigners and Chinese Christians*, pp. 149,150.

20

The Memorial Stones

'Let this be written for a future generation,
that a people not yet created may praise the LORD.'

Psalm 102:18[1]

Our surprises were not over. As we found seats around the table, one of the women produced a pile of papers she had just printed. She gave them to Zhang, who quietly sat reading them for a moment and then burst out, *'Ta zhen shi yi ge qi ji ya*! It's a miracle, it's a miracle!'

On the papers, written in Chinese, were Herbert and Elizabeth's names. The church members were asking for the BMS missionary compound by the west gate, which Herbert had planned and started to build, to be returned to their possession. This was the document they had prepared and this was the very day they intended to hand it to local government officials. The missionaries' accommodation, dispensary, school buildings and the old church were still standing, but the site now housed ninety families. The church had been praying for contact with a relative of one of the martyred missionaries. They wanted to know if there was written evidence to support their claim of ownership. I had a great sense of privilege at being there. I was in Xinzhou as part of God's plan. I was to be a small help to the church my great-grandparents had nurtured into existence through its early years of struggle.[2]

On my return to Britain, I opened the family's black tin box of documents and viewed the contents with new eyes. I began to follow Elizabeth and Herbert's steps across the last decades of the nineteenth century. I uncovered their letters to relatives and friends. I found the messages they had written to each other and to their children. Old photographs provided pictures of their appearance. Articles and books in library archives answered questions and filled in gaps. Elizabeth's orderliness and the damaging frailties of her health became apparent. Herbert's directness in his disputes with his colleagues, his dry wit and his drive to serve on the mission field became evident. Slowly, the two people I had only distantly known as my martyred great-grandparents became real people.

Herbert and Elizabeth were well supported on the mission field, particularly by the people they had carefully chosen to be the guardians of their children. They had no idea that within two years of leaving Britain in 1899 these families would be providing permanent homes for them. My great-grandparents' letters reveal their deep love for the children and made me aware of how concerned they were for their physical and spiritual welfare. Painful as it was to be parted from Benjie, Charlie, Mary and Ridley, that hard decision saved the children's lives, and gave me my own.

It became clear that I had Mary, my great-aunt, to thank for preserving the family's papers. I knew little about her. It was hard for Elizabeth to leave her only daughter in the care of a Mrs Hunt of Worthing, and heartbreaking for Mary to lose her mother. The relationship between Mary and her guardian, nevertheless, must have been a good one. Mary came to call her guardian 'Mother' and changed her surname to Hunt. In letters written during the Second World War, Benjie, Charlie and Ridley are full of affection towards their 'dearest little sister'. She was an articulate letter-writer, keeping in touch with her nieces and nephews. When, in her early twenties, Mary visited a Welsh relative, he described her as a charming and good-looking young woman. She, however, did not marry, and lived as Mrs Hunt's companion. As I rummaged through the black box, I came across her will. She died in 1952. It was one of those eureka moments. She had written: 'To my brother Thomas Benjamin or if he shall have predeceased me to his son all my Dixon family papers (at present in the black tin box in my wardrobe).'

How Herbert's diary and last messages reached the children is another miracle of this story. As I searched through my great-grandparents' papers, one Chinese name stood out – Chao, the evangelist at Xinzhou. He had recovered these precious documents. Alongside the stories told by Sowerby and Turner as they returned to Xinzhou to revive the missionary work are reports of Chao's flight to Shandong Province to get help for Herbert and the others. After a difficult, hazardous journey, he had arrived in Shandong in August 1900. When nothing was heard of the missionaries, he volunteered to return to Shanxi and refused any reward.

'The missionaries have incurred their death, or if any still survive their lives are in danger, for the sake of us Chinese, and the least we can do is risk our lives for them. As for the reward, I do not want it; if I could only be the means of saving any one of them that would be my reward'[3] he told members of the BMS.

No one could have been more fitted for the purpose. He had a deep affection and respect for the Shanxi missionaries, with whom he had worked for some eighteen years, and had an in-depth knowledge of the province and its people. However, in going back to Shanxi, he put himself in great danger. He was known as a courageous preacher and, perhaps because of his small height, more easily recognized. Having recovered the diary and other papers, he took them to Beijing. Timothy Richard, Herbert's 'adversary' of the past, made sure they were given to the children. These were the last tangible reminders of their parents.

I love the story of this man Chao. The Dixon family owe him a great debt of gratitude. Without his faith-filled bravery we would know so little of Elizabeth and Herbert's last days. After the Boxer Rebellion, Chao continued to work in Shanxi Province, where he was needed in 'gathering together the scattered remnants of the smitten flock in Shanxi',[4] and then helping the church to grow. He spent almost fifty years in Xinzhou before retiring to his hometown, aged 72. He was a loyal friend to my great-grandparents, and an excellent Chinese evangelist, highly regarded by the missionaries who worked alongside him.

Chao's story took me back to Elizabeth's final words as they parted on the track the day they fled Xinzhou: 'I have four children . . . Pray for them, Chao. Pray for them.'[5] I have no doubt that Chao did as my great-grandmother asked, though he never met the children again. My grandfather went on from his schooling to lead an interesting life. Like Herbert, he trained in medicine at University College Hospital, London. Then, rather than return to China, he set up a general practice in a deprived area of Bristol, where he gained a reputation for treating patients who could not pay for his services, or who paid in kind. He also served as captain surgeon (RNVR) in the Royal Navy in the Battle of the Falkland Islands in 1914.[6] This led to his appointment, in later life, as honorary physician to King George VI; a position he accepted with his typical humility – 'a very great honour for so mediocre a person as I know myself to be'. He and his wife, Norah, had three children. The eldest, Foster Hickman Dixon, my father, was named after Herbert and Elizabeth's Cambridge benefactor, Charles Foster, and after my grandfather's guardians, a Mr and Mrs Hickman. My grandfather's life was not without further sorrow. Having lost his parents, he also lost his son. In 1949, my father was killed while flight-testing a prototype Gyrodyne helicopter. A poorly machined link in the rotor hub failed and the machine plunged to the ground. I was nearly 4 years old; my father was 36.

While my grandfather never returned to China, Ridley and Charlie did. Ridley studied engineering at university and specialized in explosives. On his return to China, he was appointed chief consultant engineer on the Yangtze River, charged with clearing rocks and rapids that hampered shipping. Such was his reputation that he became known as 'Dynamite Dixon'. Unfortunately, conflict between local warlords cost him his living. In the Second World War, he was captured by the Japanese and spent four years in a POW camp. When the family arrived back in England, penniless and homeless, the Dixon link with China, which had lasted seventy years, came to a close.

Charlie worked as a mercantile assistant in Shanghai, but at the outbreak of the First World War returned to Britain, having been recommended for a commission, and subsequently fought in France. He then went back to China, employed by a machinery import company in Tianjin where he also served for a while on the British Municipal Council, before once again returning to Britain. He, like my grandfather, lost a son. Herbert, a pilot in the RAF, was killed during the first few months of the Second World War. Charlie and his wife, Maggie, finally emigrated to New Zealand.

In another search of the black box, I found a startling link with the past. A newspaper cutting from the *North China Herald* revealed details of a wedding in Shanghai in 1914: 'The marriage of Miss Margaret Richard, daughter of the Revd Timothy Richard, LittD, LLD, and Mr Charles Dixon, son of the Revd Herbert Dixon, took place on Saturday afternoon at the Union Church.'[7]

After the death of my great-grandparents, Richard had written a tender letter to Benjie, Charlie and Ridley, expressing his great grief at the news. He relayed a message from Herbert, 'Your father's message was that "he sent his love to his boys and he hoped they would come out as missionaries to China".' I doubt if Herbert's quarrel with Richard over his methods of missionary work was easily forgotten. However, Richard's letter to the boys shows no animosity and his autobiography is free of malice. Nonetheless, I find it difficult to believe that in the 1880s either man would have imagined that Richard would become Charlie's father-in-law!

I am glad that Richard was able to forgive my great-grand-father. Perhaps as a deliberate act of public repentance and forgiveness, the Chinese authorities and the BMS wisely held the memorial service for the Xinzhou martyrs on 'the very spot'[8] of their murders. Herbert and Elizabeth would not have wanted it any other way. Their prayer was that the people of Shanxi Province and future generations would come to know Christ and his forgiveness. When Stuart and I set out on our trip to China in 2006, I had no idea that part of God's plan in taking us to Xinzhou was to bring forgiveness for events that took place long before I was born.

As I have written, one of the great influences on the direction of Herbert's life was the prayer written by his great-grand-mother:

> It is our heart's desire and prayer that our children may be prais-ing God on earth when we are gone to praise him in heaven . . . Let not the light of our family religion be put out nor that treas-ure be buried in our graves, but let those who shall come after us do thee more and better service in their day, than we have done in ours, and be unto Thee for a name and a praise.

This prayer has had an impact on both our lives. I am as much an answer to it as my great-grandfather was. Six genera-tions after it was written, I know and love Christ. This discov-ery of faith came when I was 19 years old, and with it a strong sense of calling to the Lord's service, which has been fulfilled in a lifetime of ministry alongside my husband. We live not far from St David's, Elizabeth's birthplace, and we serve in a parish in Welsh-speaking west Wales.

When Stuart was given the opportunity for a sabbatical, he decided he wanted to study church growth in different parts of the world. We had read of the persecution of the Chinese church during the Mao years. As our plans developed, I was anxious to know what had happened to the Xinzhou church. What we discovered, as our Chinese hosts shuttled us from their office to the martyrs' memorial, to the east gate, and on to their church, was not what we expected.

The new Xinzhou church is visible a long way off. It seats over one thousand people. It has terracotta walls trimmed with white, a pink and blue metal spire, topped with a red cross, and turrets. It looks like a castle.

'Our congregation is over four thousand.'

'We have forty congregations in the towns and villages around the city.'

'This year we have already baptized 300 people. All of them over 18.'

'We want to see 10 per cent of Xinzhou's population become Christians in the next ten years.'

'But that would be 40,000 new Christians!' was my husband's stunned reply.

Such faith and vision under not the easiest of circumstances is remarkable. Here is the church the missionaries lived and died for, a church that has experienced persecution several times over the last 100 years. Inside the church, written in black characters down one side of the entrance doors are the names of the murdered missionaries; on the other side, the names of the Chinese martyrs. Christine, Stuart and I gathered with the Chinese believers in a small circle at the front of the empty church and, with Zhang as our translator, prayed together. The work of Herbert and Elizabeth came alive before my eyes. The moment took my breath away. I was filled with sheer joy.

As I look back on my journey to Xinzhou, my mind fills with memories of the memorial stones in the field above the city. I can still hear the crackling of the dead maize, picture the damaged slabs, and trace the names of my great-grandparents. I can see one of the Chinese Christians coming towards me. Her eyes are full of tears. She clutches both my hands in hers. Her head is bowed and she whispers in broken English: 'Please forgive me. Forgive us.'

Her sorrow was deep. Her feeling of shame was plain. For me, in that moment, in that place, it was so simple to forgive. I almost felt as if I didn't need to. This woman was the living testimony to my great-grandparents' faith and the fruit of their martyrdom. I told her so. Our worlds had met through the one Elizabeth and Herbert 'served unto death'. We both loved *Shijie de Jiuzhu*, the Saviour of the world. Tears flowed as I held her hands tightly and then we put our arms around each other, oblivious to everyone else. During the rest of the day, each of the Chinese church members found a way to say sorry for the brutal killing of my brave relatives. Forgiveness flowed. I cannot help but feel that God's will was done; that he was pleased at the completion of a greater plan of which I was privileged to be part.

NOTES

1 Psalm 102:18 (NIV 2011).

2 As I write these final chapters to Herbert and Elizabeth's story, I have just received an email telling me that the local government has declared the missionary compound a preserved historical site; the work of my great-grandparents and their colleagues will not be forgotten in Xinzhou.

3 Chao Xiayun, quoted in letter from J.P. Bruce to the BMS, Chefoo, 10 November 1900, quoted in 'Our Martyred Missionaries', *The Missionary Herald*, January 1901, p. 4.

4 A. Sowerby, 'Chao Hsia Yun: Evangelist', *The Missionary Herald*, April 1901, p. 139.

5 Benjamin Dixon recorded a description of his participation in the First World War, edited by his granddaughter, Rose Dixon; *The Enemy Fought Splendidly: Being the 1914–15 Diary of the Battle of the Falklands & its Aftermath*, T.B. Dixon, Blandford Press, Poole, 1983.

6 E.M. Dixon, adapted from letter from J.P. Bruce to the BMS, Chefoo, 10 November 1900, quoted in 'Our Martyred Missionaries', *The Missionary Herald*, January 1901, p. 7.

7 Adapted from *North China Herald*, Shanghai, 1914.

8 M.B. Duncan, 'Public Funeral in Honour of Our Martyred Missionaries in Hsin Chou, Shansi Province', *The Missionary Herald*, November 1901, p. 509.

Afterword

The Boxer Rebellion in Shanxi Province, 1900

On the 17 September 1900, Alfred Baynes, the general secretary of the Baptist Missionary Society in London, received a telegram. It was dated two days previous to receipt and had been sent from the treaty port of Chefoo on the north coast of Shandong Province, China. It was sent by the Reverend Robert Forsyth, one of the BMS missionaries:

Reliable educated native has brought news from Shansi [Shanxi]; Pigott party arrested Shouyang, driven on foot in chains to Tai-Yuen-Fu [Taiyuan] shared fate other missionaries. Mission houses Tai-Yuen-Fu [Taiyuan] burned, except Farthings. Missionaries fled there 29th June, escorted Yamen 9th July, promised safety, immediately massacred, altogether 33 Protestants, Pigotts 3, Duval, Robinson, Attwaters 2, Stokes 2, Simpsons 2, Lovetts 3, Coombs, Beynon 4, Wilsons 3, Farthings 5, Whitehouse 2, and four others. Hoddle Underwoods Stewart has [sic] not been mentioned, also 10 Catholic priests, others not known, probable total, 51 foreigners, besides many natives. Hsi Cho [Xinzhou] six persons escaped mountains horseback probably Dixons, McCurrachs, Renaut, Ennals, fate unknown.[1]

Two months later, on Monday, 19 November, the BMS China Committee formally logged the receipt of a second telegram from another of its missionaries, Reverend Percy Bruce, also sent from Chefoo and dated 7 November:

> Shansi messenger returned confirms Tai Yuan Fu massacre, Pigotts included; reports Dixons, McCurrachs, Underwoods, Renaut, Ennals, left Hsin Chow [Xinzhou] for cave in hills, 29th June. Boxers found them armed 31st July, and returned, not daring attack. Official went with soldiers, promised escort to coast. Missionaries, already five days without food, came out, taken to Hsin Chow [Xinzhou], imprisoned till August 9th, then killed inside City Gate.[2]

Having no reason to doubt the validity of either telegram, the committee drew its conclusions: 'It is clear therefore, that all the members of the Shansi staff of the Society, including Miss Renaut of the Zenana Mission, have been massacred . . .'[3] While there were errors in the detail, the committee's stark deduction was correct; its mission in Shanxi Province had been wiped out in its entirety. The society had lost thirteen workers in two separate incidents a month apart. Only Arthur and Louisa Sowerby, due to the fact that they were in Britain when the troubles escalated, had survived. The Shanxi devastation was in sharp contrast to the experiences of BMS communities elsewhere (ten workers in Shaanxi and thirty-six in Shandong).[4] While mission properties were looted, the missionaries of Shandong were escorted safely to the coast as early as 1 July, and the Shaanxi company all made their way to Shanghai, arriving without any fatalities in August.

The committee expressed its 'profoundest sympathy with the members of the grief-stricken families who, by these events, have been so sorely bereaved' and 'specially the four orphan children of Mr. and Mrs. Dixon'.⁵ The family of George and Catherine Farthing had been less fortunate. There were no surviving children. Ruth, Guy and Betty Farthing, aged 10, 8 and 3, perished in the massacre of missionaries at the Taiyuan *yamen* alongside their parents. Tragically, Catherine Farthing and the children had returned to China just three and a half months before their murders. Catherine Farthing had clung to her husband but George Farthing had gently released himself and knelt silently before his executioner, the first of the thirty-four missionary workers to be murdered that day. When Catherine's turn came, she was separated from her children, and then each of the family was decapitated. Reverend Frank Whitehouse and his wife were the other BMS missionaries murdered with them.

The BMS was not alone in suffering great losses in Shanxi Province. In 1880, as the Protestant missionary work in the province got underway, there were twelve missionaries, including wives, and no converts to Christianity. Eighteen years later, over one hundred and fifty missionaries, representing missions from Britain, Scandinavia and the USA, presided over a church of more than one and a half thousand members. Of over one hundred and eighty Protestant missionaries and more than fifty children killed in the Boxer Rebellion, 113 adults and 45 children came from nine missions stationed in Shanxi.⁶

The largest contingent of missionaries killed in a single day was, perhaps unsurprisingly, in the provincial capital, Taiyuan, where the governor, Yuxian, held office. The BMS missionaries in the south-east corner of the city worked alongside a representative of the British and Foreign Bible Society, the staff at the Schofield Memorial Hospital and an independent worker. By the north gate there was a Roman Catholic compound with a cathedral capable of seating 1,000, a training seminary for Chinese converts, and a girls' orphanage, run by two bishops, two priests, a lay worker and seven Sisters of Mercy. On 9 July, forty-five people, including the Farthings, the Whitehouses, and missionaries serving in other cities who had been brought to the provincial capital, met their deaths, among them eleven children and the twelve Roman Catholics. Yuxian himself supervised the killings within the *yamen* precincts. The missionaries were ordered to name their country of origin and were then put to the sword. One of the Roman Catholic bishops, an elderly man, remonstrated with Yuxian. The governor slashed him across the face with his sword so that blood ran down over the bishop's large white beard. Then he was killed. The wife of Dr Arnold Lovitt, a medic at the hospital, holding her young son, John, by his hand, asked, 'We all came to China to bring you the good news of salvation by Jesus Christ. We have done you no harm, but only sought your good; why do you treat us so?'[7] There was no answer. A soldier took off her spectacles and both mother and son were killed.

The governor was fêted by citizens of Taiyuan for his actions, and a stone tablet set up to celebrate 'his achievements in clearing the province of the hated foreigners'.[8] But Yuxian's 'triumph' was short-lived. In the aftermath of the Boxer Rebellion, Yuxian was dispensed with by Cixi in response to the demands of foreign governments. He was informed by the Beijing court that 'the price of coffins is rising'[9] and his execution ordered (though there remains doubt as to whether this was in fact carried out). Ironically, it is reported that when the Qing Dynasty was overthrown in the revolution of 1911, Yuxian's daughter found refuge with missionaries of the BMS to escape the slaughter of the deposed Manchu rulers.

Amongst the many paragraphs relating the stories of foreign missionaries, which were written at the time in missionary reports and books, are sentences about the fate of Chinese believers. After the death of the Roman Catholic bishops at Taiyuan, the cathedral was attacked the following day and forty-nine adherents massacred. In a village close to the provincial capital, the Roman Catholic church lost 200 members. Other stories were collected in more detail by the first missionaries to return to Shanxi. The death of Old He at Xinzhou was one of many tragic tales recorded. Two sisters-in-law at Fanshi, north of Xinzhou, were condemned to death, one for carrying poison for wells, the other for cutting out bewitched paper men to create trouble in the city. Wang, a 33-year-old gambler and opium smoker converted to Christianity, and an unmistakably reformed character as a result, was offered the opportunity to abandon the 'foreign religion'. He refused, telling his persecutors, 'I now follow the heavenly doctrine, reverence *Shangdi*, the supreme ruler, believe in Jesus, and worship the true God. How can you say I belong to a foreign sect? I have left the foreign sect to follow Jesus.'[10] After much argument, the Boxers declared that his mind had been poisoned by the missionaries, and took Wang outside the city gates for execution.

There are no final figures for the number of Chinese Christian deaths that occurred in the Boxer Rebellion, or an inventory of the destruction and looting of their homes. It is estimated that around two thousand Chinese Protestants were killed across China. Of over two hundred members of the BMS Shanxi church, 120 were lost. The Roman Catholic Church fared far worse. In Shanxi, around eight thousand members were murdered. In total, approximately thirty thousand adherents were lost, though fewer of their foreign priests and nuns (forty) were killed.

What is true is that each of these stories, known or unknown, is as great a tragedy as the deaths of Elizabeth and Herbert Dixon. The faithfulness of so many Chinese Christians in the face of persecution, and their courageous refusal to accept the simple painless option of recanting, are testimony that they were not the 'rice Christians' they were so readily accused of being, but genuine believers as faithful as the missionaries who had travelled across the world to serve them and who died alongside them.

No doubt, over a hundred years later, tucked away in churches and chapels, there are still small reminders of the men, women and children who died in the Boxer Rebellion. Herbert and Elizabeth share a place on the Missionary Roll of Honour at Downs Chapel on the edge of Hackney Common in London. Elizabeth also has her own memorial, written in Welsh, in distinct black script on white marble, prominently displayed on the wall to the left of the pulpit of the Tabernacle Chapel in St David's, Wales:

Er Cof Am
Elizabeth, merch Thomas
ac Elizabeth Williams, Clegyr,
a Magedig yn yr Eglwys hon.
llofruddiwyd hi a'i phriod, Y
Parch Herbert Dixon, ar faes Cenhadol
China. Awst 1900.

———

"Dy Ferthyr Di."

A translation reads:

In Memory Of
Elizabeth, daughter of Thomas
and Elizabeth Williams, Clegyr,
Brought up in this Church.
She was murdered, with her husband, The
Revd Herbert Dixon, on the Mission Field
China. August 1900.

———

"Your Martyr."

NOTES

[1] Minutes of the BMS China Committee, September 1900, p. 250.
[2] Minutes of the BMS China Committee, September 1900, p. 255.
[3] Ibid.
[4] The ten workers in Shaanxi included two members of the Baptist Zenana Mission. One of the BMS wives was in Britain. There were thirty-six workers in Shandong Province, of which six were

members of the Baptist Zanana Mission. Of these thirty-six, two couples, two of the wives and one member of the Baptist Zanana Mission were in Britain. It is possible that some but not necessarily all of those in Britain had left earlier than planned due to the growing tensions.

5   Minutes of the BMS China Committee, September 1900, p. 255.

6   China Inland Mission – 47 workers/16 children; CMA – 21/15, BMS – 13/3; American Board – 10/5; Shouyang Mission – 11/2; Scandinavian Alliance Mongolian Mission 5/0; BFBS – 2/3; Swedish Mongolian Mission – 3/1; Independent 1/0.

7   Mrs Lovitt, quoted in R.C. Forsyth, *The China Martyrs of 1900*, pp. 38,39.

8   A.H. Smith, *China in Convulsion, Vol. 2* (New York, Chicago, Toronto: Fleming H. Revell, 1901), p. 615.

9   P. Fleming, *The Siege at Peking* (London: Arrow Books, 1962), p. 242.

10 Wang Xin, adapted from E.H. Edwards, *Fire and Sword in Shansi: The Story of the Martyrdom of Foreigners and Chinese Christians*, p. 195.

Special Memorial Service
COMMEMORATIVE OF THE
MARTYRDOM
OF THE
SHANSI MISSIONARIES
OF
The Baptist Missionary Society.
BLOOMSBURY CHAPEL,
THURSDAY, DECEMBER 13th, 1900.
"*They loved not their lives unto the death.*"

Author's Notes

Material for this book has been drawn from a wide variety of sources – some modern reflections on the periods described, others written nearer to the time. Quotations are referenced and a bibliography of the main sources of material provided. Quotations from letters and documents held in the Dixon family private collection have not been referenced. In some instances, quotations, particularly quotations from letters, have been 'tidied up', e.g. spelling and grammar corrected, or shortened for ease of reading, but no alteration has been made to the sense of the original quotation. Where quotations from published sources have been adapted, this has been noted.

The spelling of Kikongo words is consistent with those used by Bentley and his colleagues during their development of the Kikongo dictionaries. The modern Pinyin romanization system has been used throughout the main text for Chinese words and place names and in quotations. Original romanized spellings have been retained for reference sources and in the Afterword (e.g. Shansi for Shanxi [Pinyin]; Hsin Chow and similar for Xinzhou [Pinyin]). Identifying Chinese place names and surnames is not always possible where sources do not provide the names in characters. Therefore some of the

Pinyin names given are based on the possible Pinyin equivalents of older romanization systems.

There are no invented characters in the story, but it has been necessary to protect the identity of people living in China. Reported conversations are imagined except where these are taken from quoted sources. The taking of dramatic licence, interpretation of facts and the style of presentation, remain my responsibility.

Ronald Clements

Glossary

Wales

Allt Felyn Fawr: *aLLt veleen vowr*

bara dan cidl: *bara dan keedl*

blaenoriaid: *bluynoreeuyd*

Brad y Llyfrau Gleision: *brad uh LLuhvruy glayseeon*

Clegyr Isaf: *klegeer eesav*

gadael i'r toes ganu: *gadel eer toys ganee*

Glyn Rhosyn: *glin rhoseen*

Dala Cwentin: *dala kooenteen*

golchbren: *golchbren*

gwahoddwr: *gooahothoor*

Gwastad Chapel: *gooastad*

hebrwng asgwrn: *hebroong asgoorn*

Llys-y-frân: *LLees-uh-vran*

mae'r sucan yn ffrwtian, bois: *muy'r seekan uhn frooteean, boees*

peidiwch â boddi'r melinydd: *paydeeooch a bothee'r melineeth*

Porthclais: *porTHkluys*

Treginnis Uchaf: *tregeenees eeCHav*

Further information on the pronunciation of Welsh may be found at http://www.bbc.co.uk/wales/livinginwales/.

China

Baoding: *b-(h)ow-ding*

Caozhang: *ts-(h)ow-j-ang*

Chao Xiayun(Chao Hsia Yun): *ch-(h)ow-she-ah-you-ne*

Chefoo (now called Yantai): *chee-foo/Yen-tie*

Chengdu: *ch-ung-do*

Cixi: *ts-she*

Daixian: *die-shen*

Daizhou (Tai-chou): *die-j-oh*

Fanshi (Fan Shih): *fan-sher*

feng shui: *f-ung-sh-way*

Fuzhou: *foo-j-oh*

Gaocheng (Chao Mon Chong): *g-(h)ow-ch-ung*

Guoxian (Kuo Hsien): *g-w-oh-shen*

Guoyangzhen: *g-w-oh-y-ang-j-hun*

Hebei Province: *he(r)-bay*

huoche: *h-w-oh-ch-er*

Jidu Jiao: *jee-do-jee-(h)ow*

Liujiashan: *lee-oh-jee-ah-shan*

Li Pengheng: *lee-p-ung-h-ung*

Pingyao: *ping-y-(h)ow*

Qicun (Chi Ts'un): *chee-t-sun*

Qing Dynasty: *ch-ing*

Qingzhou: *ch-ing-j-oh*

sha: *sh-ah*

Shaanxi Province: *shan-she*

Shangdi (the supreme ruler/God): *sh-ang-dee*

Shanghai: *sh-ang-hi*

Shandong: *shan-dong*

Shanxi Province: *shan-she*

shao: *sh-(h)ow*
Shijie de Jiuzhu: *sher-jee-ay-de-jee-oh-j-(w)oo*
Shouyang: *sh-oh-y-ang*
Sun Wukong: *sun-woo-kong*
Taihang Mountains: *tie-h-ang*
Taitai (the Chinese word for wife and a term of respect to older women): *tie-tie*
Taiyuan: *tie-you-(h)en*
Tianjin: *t-yen-jee-in*
Wang Xin: *w-ang-shin*
Xiahebei: *she-ah-he(r)-bay*
Xian: *she-an*
Xinzhou: *shin-j-oh*
Wen Chang: *w-un-ch-ang*
yamen: *yeah-mun*
yang guizi: *y-ang-g-way-z-er*
Yangtze River: *y-ang-see*
Yihetuan: *ee- he(r)-to-wan*
Yiheyuan: *ee- he(r)-you-(h)en*
Yuxian: *you-shen*
zheng: *j-(h)ung*
Zhu Bajie: *j-(w)oo-ba-jee-ay*

Further information on the pronunciation of Mandarin Pinyin may be found at http://www.ctcfl.ox.ac.uk.

Bibliography

Wales

Beddoe, D. *Out of the Shadows: A History of Women in Twentieth-Century Wales* (Cardiff: University of Wales Press, 2000).

Davies, P.B.S. *The Footsteps of our Fathers: Tales of Life in Nineteenth Century St. David's* (St David's: Merrivale Publications, 1994).

Evans, H. *Twr-y-felin: History and Guide to St. David's,* 2nd edn (St David's, Twr-y-Felin Hotel: private publication, 1923).

Howell, D.W., ed. *Pembrokeshire County History: Volume IV: Modern Pembrokeshire 1815–1874* (Haverfordwest: The Pembrokeshire Historical Society, 1993).

John, A.V., ed. *Our Mother's Land: Chapters in Welsh Women's History 1830–1939* (Cardiff: University of Wales Press, 1991).

Middleton, G.W. *The Streets of St. David's* (St David's: The St. David's Civic Society, Yr Oriel Fach Press, 1977).

Thomas, J.M. *Looking Back: A Childhood in Saint David's a Century Ago* (St David's: Merrivale Publications, 1999).

Tibbott, S.M. and B. Thomas, eds. *Domestic Life in Wales* (Cardiff: University of Wales Press, 2002).

Reports of the Commissioners of Inquiry into the State of Education in Wales: Part 1: Carmarthen, Glamorgan and Pembroke (London: Her Majesty's Stationery Office,1847).

Liverpool

Jones, R.M. and D.B. Rees. *Liverpool Welsh & Their Religion* (Liverpool: Modern Welsh Publications, 1984).

Stanley, D., ed. *The Autobiography of Sir Henry Morton Stanley* (Boston and New York: Houghton Mifflin Company, 1909).

London

Abel-Smith, B. *A History of the Nursing Profession* (London: Heinemann, 1960).

Alvey, N. *Education by Election: Reed's School, Clapton and Watford* (St Albans: St Albans and Hertfordshire Architectural and Archaeological Society, 1990).

—. 'The London Orphan Asylum'. *Terrier* (1991), pp. 2–4.

Anon. 'Nurses and Doctors', *British Medical Journal* (17 January 1880), p. 97.

Baker, T.F.T. and C.R. Elrington, eds. *A History of the County of Middlesex: Volume 8 – Islington and Stoke Newington Parishes* (1985) http://www.british-history.ac.uk/catalogue.aspx?gid=66 (accessed 29 October 2013).

Baker, T.F.T., ed. *A History of the County of Middlesex: Volume 10 – Hackney* (1995) http://www.british-history.ac.uk/catalogue.aspx?gid=66 (accessed 29 October 2013).

Black, N. 'Rise and Demise of the Hospital: a Reappraisal of Nursing'. *British Medical Journal* 10/331(7529)(December 2005), pp. 1394–96.

Bynum, W.E. *Science and the Practice of Medicine in the Nineteenth Century* (Cambridge: Cambridge University Press, 1994).

Domville, E.J. *A Manual for Hospital Nurses and Others Engaged in Attending the Sick* (London: J. & A. Churchill, 1875).

Francis, J.E. 'Fifty Years Ago. A Round with Mr Christopher Heath'. *UCH Magazine* 34 (July 1949), pp. 69–72.

Hawkins, S. *Nursing and Women's Labour in the Nineteenth Century: The Quest for Independence* (London and New York: Routledge, 2010).

Hearnshaw, F.J.C. *The Centenary History of King's College London, 1828–1928* (London: George G. Harrap, 1929).

Holloway, S.W.F. 'The All Saints' Sisterhood at University College Hospital 1862–99'. *Medical History* 3(2) (April 1959), pp. 146–156.

Horton, P. *The London Orphan Asylum (Clapton 1825–1871): Notes for a History* (unpublished manuscript, Hackney Archives, London, ca. 1960–68).

Jones, E., ed. *The Welsh in London 1500–2000* (Cardiff: University of Wales Press, 2001).

Likeman, J. 'Nursing at University College Hospital, London, 1862–1948: from Christian Vocation to Secular Profession'. (Unpublished doctoral thesis, University of London, Institute of Education, 2002).

Mayhew, H. *London Labour and the London Poor: Vol. 3, The London Street-Folk; comprising, Street sellers. Street buyers. Street finders. Street performers. Street artizans. Street labourers* (London: Griffin, Bohn, and Company, 1861).

—. *London Labour and the London Poor: Vol. 4, Those that will not work; comprising, Prostitutes. Thieves. Swindlers. Beggars* (London: Griffin, Bohn, and Company, 1862).

—. *London Street Life: Selections of the Writings of Henry Mayhew* (Queen's Classics, London: Chatto and Windus Educational, 1966).

Merrington, W.R. *University College Hospital and its Medical School: a History* (London: Heinemann, 1976).

Mumm, S., ed. *All Saints Sisters of the Poor: An Anglican Sisterhood in the 19th Century* (Church of England Record Society no. 9, Woodbridge, Suffolk: The Boydell Press, 2001).

—. *Stolen Daughters, Virgin Mothers: Anglican Sisterhoods in Victorian Britain* (London: Leicester University Press, 1999).

Nightingale, Florence. *Report of the Committee Appointed to Consider the Cubic Space of Metropolitan Workhouses* (London: Her Majesty's Stationery Office, 1867).

Norton, G. *Victorian London* (London: MacDonald, 1969).

Peterson, M.J. *The Medical Profession in Mid-Victorian London* (Berkeley, Los Angeles, London: University of California Press, 1978).

Pope-Hennessy, J. *Queen Mary, 1867–1953* (London: George Allen and Unwin, 1959).

Reed, A. and C. Reed. *Memoirs of the Life and Philanthropic Labours of Andrew Reed D.D.* (London: Strahan and Co., 1863).

Reed's School, Cobham. 'Archive of the Secretary to the Governors, 1814–1988' http://www.cxploringsurrcyspast .org.uk/GetRecord/SHCOL_3719_(PART1OF2) (accessed 6 February 2012).

Richardson, J. *The Annals of London: a Year-by-Year Record of a Thousand Years of History* (London: Weidenfield & Nicolson Illustrated, 2001).

Shaw, I.J. *The Greatest is Charity* (Darlington: Evangelical Press, 2005).

Victorian Pharmacy, Episodes 1–4 (BBC2, 15 July, 22 July, 5 August, 12 August, 2010).

Congo

Bentley, W.H. *Appendix to the Dictionary and Grammar of the Kongo Language: As Spoken at San Salvador, the Ancient Capital of the Old Kongo Empire, West Africa* (London: Baptist Missionary Society and Kegan Paul, Trench, Trübner and Company, 1895).

—. *Life on the Congo* (London: The Religious Tract Society, 1887).

—. *Pioneering on the Congo: Volumes 1 and 2* (New York: Fleming H. Revell, 1900).

Cox, F.A. *History of the Baptist Missionary Society, from 1792 to 1842: to which is added a sketch of the General Baptist Mission, Volumes 1 and 2* (London: T. Ward and Co. and G. and J. Dyer, 1842).

Hawker, G. *The Life of George Grenfell* (New York: Fleming H. Revell, 1909).

Hemmens, H.L. *George Grenfell: Pioneer in Congo (London: Student Christian Movement*, 1927).

Johnston, H.H. *George Grenfell and the Congo: Volumes 1 and 2* (London: Hutchinson, 1908).

—. *The River Congo from its Mouth to Bolobo with a General Description of the Natural History and Anthropology of its Western Basin* (London: Sampson Low, Marston, 1895).

Kivilu, S. 'Mantantu Dundulu: 1865 to 1938' *Dictionary of African Christian Biography* http://www.dacb.org/stories/demrepcongo/mantantu_dundulu.html (accessed 29 October 2013).

The Missionary Herald, Baptist Missionary Society.

Stanley, B. *The History of the BMS 1792–1992* (Edinburgh: T & T Clark, 1992).

China

'A Portsmouth Missionary in China', *Hampshire Telegraph and Sussex Chronicle* (9 May 1885).

Broomhall, M., ed. *Martyred Missionaries of the China Inland Mission, with a Record of the Perils and Sufferings of Some who Escaped* (London: Morgan and Scott, 1901).

Edwards, E.H. *Fire and Sword in Shansi: The Story of the Martyrdom of Foreigners and Chinese Christians* (Edinburgh and London: Oliphant Anderson and Ferrier, 1903).

Fleming, P. *The Siege at Peking* (London: Arrow Books, 1962).

Forsyth, R.C. *The China Martyrs of 1900* (London: The Religious Tract Society, 1904).

Grubb, N. *C.T. Studd: Cricketer and Pioneer* (Guildford and London: Lutterworth Press, 1970).

Kaiser, A.T. *A History of Protestant Missions in Shanxi* (unpublished manuscript, 2006).

The Missionary Herald, Baptist Missionary Society.

Preston, D. *The Boxer Rebellion: The Dramatic Story of China's War on Foreigners that Shook the World in the*

Summer of 1900 (New York: The Berkley Publishing Group, 1999/2000).

Purcell, V. *The Boxer Uprising* (Cambridge: Cambridge University Press, 1963).

Richard, T. *Forty-five Years in China* (New York: Frederick A. Stokes, 1916).

Smith, A.H. *China in Convulsion*, Vol. 2 (New York, Chicago, Toronto: Fleming H. Revell, 1901).

Smith, K.E. 'Women in Cultural Captivity: British Women and the Zenana Mission'. *Baptist Heritage and History* 41/1 (Winter 2006), pp. 30–41.

Soothill, W.E. *Timothy Richard of China: Seer, Statesman, Missionary and the Most Disinterested Adviser the Chinese Ever Had* (London: Seeley, Service, 1924).

Stanley, B. *The History of the BMS 1792–1992* (Edinburgh: T & T Clark, 1992).

Turner, F.S. *British Opium Policy and its Results to India and China* (London: Sampson Low, Marston, Searle and Rivington, 1976).

Williamson, H.R. *British Baptists in China 1845–1952* (London: The Carey Kingsgate Press, 1957).